SMARTER BRANDING

BRANDING

Without Breaking The Bank

Five Proven Marketing Strategies You Can Use Right Now
to Build Your Business at Little or No Cost

Brenda Bence

INTERNATIONAL BRANDING EXPERT AND COACH

Global
Insight

Published by Global Insight Communications LLC, Las Vegas, Nevada, U.S.A.

ISBN: 978-0-9825353-1-8
Library of Congress Control Number: 2011935252

Cover design by George Foster, Foster Covers (www.fostercovers.com)
Interior design and typesetting by Eric Myhr

The stories and examples in this book are based on real events, real companies, and real people. Where requested, and in order to protect the privacy of certain individuals, names and identifying details have been changed.

The author and the publisher do not make any claim of copyright for the brands, logos, and other advertisements discussed throughout the book. Those materials belong to their respective owners. The discussion/commentary regarding any brands or other copyrighted materials are for purposes of illustration, analysis, or comment only. The author's comments and analyses are entirely her own, based on extensive branding experience, and were not done in consultation with any of the companies or brands represented. The purpose of the illustrations and analyses is to help educate business leaders and entrepreneurs to improve their own business knowledge with respect to branding and marketing and to assist them in better communicating their brands to the marketplace.

Limit of Liability/Disclaimer of Warrant: While the publisher and author have used their best efforts in preparing this book, they make no representations or warranties with respect to the accuracy or completeness of the contents of this book and specifically disclaim any implied warranties of merchantability or fitness for a particular purpose. No warranty may be created or extended by sales representatives or written sales materials. The advice and strategies contained herein may not be suitable for your own specific situation. Neither the publisher nor author shall be liable for any loss of profit or any other commercial damages as a result of the suggestions made in this book, including but not limited to, special, incidental, consequential, or other damages.

Publisher's Cataloging-in-Publication Data:

Bence, Brenda S.
    Smarter branding without breaking the bank : five marketing strategies you can use right now to build your business at little or no cost /
Brenda Bence.
    p. cm.
    ISBN 978-0-9825353-1-8
1. Branding (Marketing). 2. Marketing. 3. Marketing --Management.
4. Advertising. 5. Entrepreneurship. I. Title.

HF5415 .B 46 2011
658.8--dc22   2011935252

This book is dedicated to
Smarter Branding Without Breaking the Bank workshop
participants from all around the globe who have
openly shared their branding challenges and dreams.

CONTENTS

INTRODUCTION

You Don't Need Deep Pockets to Build a Strong Brand

"A brand is a living entity—and it is enriched or undermined cumulatively over time, the product of a thousand small gestures."
— MICHAEL EISNER, FORMER CEO OF DISNEY

A FEW YEARS AGO, *Time* magazine reported that the average American living in a large urban city runs across 3,000 brands every single day. That's a lot by anyone's estimation. Now, if you're a business owner or someone responsible for building a brand, that can be mighty intimidating. How do you get customers to notice your offering in an endless sea of other brands?

You may even feel that you don't have the resources to think about branding because you're just trying to keep your company afloat. Or you might feel that you just aren't in a position to grow beyond where you are right now. After all, if you're only bringing in so much profit, how much can you put back into marketing without going into serious debt? Without the budget of a Fortune 500 company, you may feel stuck and unable to move forward. If that sounds like you, trust me—you aren't alone.

But here's the good news: I'm here to tell you that you absolutely *can* build a brand without deep pockets. And, contrary to what a lot of news announcers will tell you, the state of the economy doesn't matter either. Up economy, down economy, flat economy, local economy, foreign economy—it just doesn't matter. It also makes no difference if you're building your brand on your own as a solo-preneur, whether you have just a few staff members, or whether you're running a company of 500 employees. The type of business is of no import either — service business, product-focused business, or both. Where you are in the process of building your brand is also irrelevant — whether you are just getting started or trying to grow a brand that has been around for a while.

Whatever your situation, you *can* successfully build your brand. You can even surpass brands that are bigger and have larger budgets. All it takes is knowing where to look, and that's what this book is about.

So What Do I Know About Building a Brand, Anyway?

Back when dinosaurs roamed the earth and a "virus" was something taken care of by a medical doctor, not an IT specialist, I got my MBA from Harvard Business School. (Okay, there weren't really dinosaurs roaming the Earth, but it was a fairly long time ago…)

Once armed with my MBA, I wanted to learn about building brands. So, I took a gamble and joined Procter & Gamble with the intent of staying just long enough to gain some insight into the marketing world and move on. What I didn't anticipate was how much I was going to love brand building! Much to my surprise, I ended up staying in brand management for a long time. In fact, I spent the next several years helping to build multi-million dollar brands for Procter & Gamble across the United States, Europe, and Asia. You've probably heard of some of the brands I worked on — Pantene Pro-V, Head & Shoulders, Vidal Sassoon, Tide, Cheer, and Ariel, just to name a few. It was a great experience because it taught me what makes big brands tick, what gets those brands to the top, and what helps them stay there.

Then, along came Bristol-Myers Squibb and, like the Godfather, they made me an offer I just couldn't refuse. I ended up becoming Vice President of International Marketing for their Consumer Division, Mead Johnson, which develops and markets children's and infants' nutritional products. If you're a parent, maybe you've heard of Enfamil? Well, that was one of the many brands I worked on during my time at BMS, and I had the incredible opportunity of managing brands across four continents and almost 50 countries. I had a great time — and learned a tremendous amount — flying around the world building the company's multi-billion dollar brands.

Taking the Plunge

But then, it happened: The "bug" bit me. You know the one — the "I-want-to-start-my-own-company" bug? (If you're reading this book, maybe you've been bitten by that bug, too.) I set about thinking how I could make that happen. I loved training, coaching, and speaking, and I wanted to find a way to combine these activities with my burning passion for branding so that I could help other people build their brands as well.

So, after more than two decades working in multi-billion dollar corporations, I took the plunge and left the security of a full-time, six-figure job. I traded it in to pursue the dream of starting my own business. I was excited!

BUT...

Along with the excitement came this ever-present undertow of ... *dread*. After all, I suddenly went from having extremely deep pockets that I could rely on to manage and build brands in the corporate world to having nearly empty pockets to build my own brand. Okay, okay — my pockets weren't *completely* empty. I did have some savings. But I really didn't want to blow my entire retirement fund on building my own brand. I knew I had to spend funds wisely if my business was going to survive. And I had to get smart — fast — about how to do that.

Faced with this dilemma, I took a deep breath and gathered up all the tips, tools, and techniques I had learned during those many years of big-brand management. I began applying them diligently to building my own brand — but this time, in ways that didn't cost much. I kept my eye on the target — on the brand I wanted to build — and that brand became the North Star to guide every day-to-day decision I made. Slowly but surely, I uncovered hundreds of ways to build my brand using the same methods I had employed with household name brands, but without the need for the deep pockets I had in the corporate world. Over time, I discovered that it was not only *possible* to build my brand without spending a mint, but that it was a lot of *fun*, too.

Fortunately, as they say, the rest is history.

The business grew to the point where I took on a number of employees, and — five years into it — my husband quit his job and joined as a partner, as well. At the time of this writing — almost ten years later — our brand has had the privilege of serving some of the world's largest, most respected companies across the globe. Our clients hail from 25 countries on six continents, and we have expanded to the point of having offices in both the U.S. and Asia. And we accomplished all of this with very limited investment. I won't share the nitty-gritty details of how much money was spent, but let me put it this way: Not long ago, we hired a second-year MBA student from Harvard Business School to intern with us for the summer. When she saw our investment figures, she was surprised to learn how little we had spent to build such a strong brand from scratch. There's absolutely no reason you can't do the same!

Taking My Knowledge "On the Road"

Once the success of both my company and my personal brand began to gain visibility, fellow entrepreneurs started asking me: "Brenda, how did you do that? What are your secrets?" Enough requests came in that I figured there must be demand for this kind of information. So, a few years ago, I agreed to lead a workshop for business owners during which I shared dozens of the powerful, low-cost branding secrets I had discovered. The goal of the workshop was to help fellow business owners learn to apply those same strategies to their own brands and catapult their companies into more profitable growth.

The first workshop was a grand success, and the word soon spread. I started doing more and more workshops, and before I knew it, demand had expanded to other countries, too. Suddenly, I found myself flying around the globe, sharing this program and my system. As a result, I've had the amazing opportunity to help thousands of small-to-medium business owners build successful brands around the world.

Workshop requests still haven't stopped coming in (which is great!), but that also makes me acutely aware of how limited I am by such mundane issues as time and space — like the fact that there are only 24 hours in a day and only one me. Ah, those dratted human constraints!

That was the impetus behind writing *Smarter Branding Without Breaking the Bank* — the book.[1] Based on my popular workshop, the

---

1. Visit www.Smarter-Branding.com for information about our accelerated brand-building program, *Fast Track to Smarter Branding*™ — *The Ultimate Package*. This one-of-a-kind course is filled with additional tools and tips to help you earn even bigger profits for less money — in less time. It includes a

goal of this book is to help business owners build a strong brand quickly and effectively — without having to spend a lot of money.

What You Will Learn

What will you get out of this book? In the pages that follow, I'll walk you through proven strategies I've discovered over the years that, first, helped me grow and build my own brand and, later, helped all types of SMEs, entrepreneurs, and solo-preneurs — regardless of size, industry, or country — to create successful brands on a shoestring budget. Here's just a little bit of what you'll discover as you read on:

- The five existing marketing assets that your company *already has at your disposal* that can help you build a strong brand.

- Ways to leverage those assets to develop and implement *low-cost* or *no-cost* business-building marketing and branding ideas.

- How to develop a six-element Brand Positioning Statement that will help you to laser-focus your marketing efforts.

- How to determine what's good and what's bad for your own specific brand — and how to stay focused on the good.

- The surprising truth about who is *really* responsible for marketing your brand.

- How to instill a "marketing mindset" in every member of your team — even if you consider yourself a one-person show.

- How to "bust" several widely held branding myths that could be holding you back from success. After reading this book, you will never fall prey to these limiting myths again.

- How to grow *yourself* into a smarter marketer, smarter brander, and smarter business leader.

20-session Video Learning Course featuring Brenda Bence; an accompanying workbook of brand-building exercises in both hard copy and fill-in-the-blank digital format; 52 new, unique, and actionable *Smarter Branding* tips emailed to you each week for a year; copies of *Smarter Branding Without Breaking the Bank* in e-book, downloadable audiobook, and paperback format; and a no-questions-asked, money-back satisfaction guarantee.

How to Use This Book

In order to get the most out of this book, decide which brand you want to focus on. Do you want to concentrate on a particular *product* brand you offer? A *service* brand? Or do you want to focus on the brand of your entire company? Perhaps your brand is your own name. Make that choice now.

Then, keep that specific brand in mind and apply it whenever you read the words "your brand" throughout these chapters. You can always go back and work on another brand later. But first, choose the most important brand for your business right now, and start there. Learning how to focus is a vital part of the process.

As with any learning process, the more you put into it, the more you will get out of it. So, I encourage you to work diligently, step-by-step, through this program. Remember: What you focus on grows. Give your brand the attention it deserves, and you will reap the rewards, both in terms of greater personal satisfaction *and* increased revenues.

Final Chance to "De-Plane"

Now, if all of this is not what you expected from this book, well … just like they say as you board an aircraft, this is your last chance to "de-plane." Otherwise, strap yourself in, and let's take off. Get ready to discover how to create your very own powerhouse brand while keeping your bank account intact.

1

KNOW YOUR "BRAND-SPEAK"

Key Branding Terms & Developing a "Marketing Mindset"

"Nothing can stop the man with the right mental attitude from achieving his goal; nothing on earth can help the man with the wrong mental attitude."

— THOMAS JEFFERSON, FORMER U.S. PRESIDENT

IN ALL MY YEARS as a marketer and brander, I've seen a lot of confusion out there about what certain marketing and branding terms really mean. I think it comes from the fact that so many of these terms aren't as simple as they may seem at first.

Case in point: Even with all my experience in the field, I've had to stop at times and consider certain definitions. Early in my days of working overseas with Proctor & Gamble, I flew home to the U.S. for a vacation. Catching up with family, I was sharing some stories about my job when my then 8-year-old niece turned to me and asked, "Aunt Brenda, what is 'marketing'?" To be perfectly honest, I was at a loss for words! (Kids ask the best questions, don't they?) At the time, I stumbled through some kind of limp response. But that episode got me thinking...how *would* I describe marketing and branding to an 8-year-old in a way that makes each word easily understood, unique, and distinctive?

The definitions you'll read in this chapter stem from that original exchange, and since you're here to build a strong brand, it's key to get some clarity around them.

What is a "Brand"?

I'm going to use the term "your brand" throughout this book, but as I mentioned in the last chapter, it's up to you which brand you want to focus on. Maybe for you, your brand refers to your entire company or perhaps to a specific product brand that you want to focus on — something tangible that you can market, like a toy or your brand of clothing. Or maybe it's a service brand if you run a business such as a restaurant, hotel, or law firm.

Whatever your specific brand represents, keep in mind that *every* brand goes beyond just the physical attributes of the product or service you offer. In fact, all brands have this much in common — they are *intangible*. Think about it: You can smell the aroma of a Starbucks cup of coffee, you can taste the flavor of a Mentos in your mouth, you can feel an ice-cold can of Sprite in your hand, you can hear the sound of Windows starting up on your computer, and you can see the golden arches of McDonald's. But you cannot *touch* a brand. You can only touch the actual product and experience the services associated with that brand. The brand itself is something that only exists in your mind.

Even though brands are "untouchable," they can still have immense power and be very influential. Take Coca-Cola, for example. Around the globe, people buy an estimated $15 billion of Coke every single year. That's more than $1 billion per month and more than the GDP of 85 countries in the world! How's *that* for powerful?

What's most important about brands is that they have both rational and emotional appeal. They provide a multi-sensory experience for customers which, in turn, creates a strong perception of added value. That's what leads to the kind of customer loyalty you are aiming for.

Let's return to Coke again. I know many Coke drinkers wouldn't dream of switching to Pepsi — and vice versa. I've even witnessed people arguing about which brand is better, despite the fact that the two brands' product ingredients are fundamentally the same. Now, *that's* brand loyalty!

Can you imagine your brand inspiring that kind of loyalty in your customers? It's entirely possible. You may not create it on the same scale as Coke or Pepsi, but by harnessing your brand correctly, you *can* absolutely create loyal customers who will stick with your brand for years to come.

What is "Branding"?

Okay, so you know what a brand is, but how does that differ from "brand*ing*"? Branding actually refers to the design elements that a brand uses to identify itself. Think logos, icons, slogans, colors, layouts, and schemes that are used consistently wherever that brand name appears. These elements might even be legally protected to make sure they are only associated with that particular brand and no other.

Think Nike's "swoosh" logo and American Express' "Don't leave home without it" tagline. That is "branding."

What is "Marketing"?

Now, to the definition that started me thinking about all of this in the first place. Here's how I like to define Marketing:

All the activities associated with identifying the specific wants and needs of a particular group of customers, and then taking action to satisfy those customers better than competition.

What I like most about this definition is that it's all about the customer. You must have a well-defined target market and make sure everything you do satisfies that target's needs better than your competitors. That's how you create brand loyalty and become the brand of choice for your customers. (We'll talk about dozens of ways to accomplish that before you finish this book.)

Now, you may think I'm a bit biased, but I actually believe Marketing is the most important function in any company. Think about it: Without customers, you have no revenues. Without revenues, you have no business. And since your marketing efforts are all about identifying the needs of your customers and filling those needs, what could be more important than that?

Marketing vs. Sales

If you're one of those people who believe Marketing and Sales are one and the same, think again. That's a common misconception, but there's a definite reason why Marketing and Sales are treated as two different functions in most companies.

An easy way to get to the bottom of the difference between the two is to ask, "Which comes first — Marketing or Sales?" Once you think of it in those terms, it really isn't a "chicken or egg" dilemma at all.

Sales is the actual customer purchase / transaction, while Marketing is what happens that leads up to that transaction.

Marketing consists of all the activities that set into motion how the sales transaction should take place, and the message communicated during that transaction is based on the marketing strategy.

So, Sales must be in sync with Marketing in order for your brand message to work. Otherwise, your customers are bound to get confused about what you stand for. We'll talk more specifically about that later but, for now, just remember that your marketing efforts are the basis upon which Sales communicates your brand message to your customers.

What is "Good" Marketing?

As you walk down a street with commercial businesses and offices in the city where you live — much like the Champs Élysées in Paris or Michigan Avenue in Chicago — you see hundreds of brand signs … and you look at some while ignoring others. You leaf through a magazine and see dozens of print ads; some have the power to make you stop and look; some don't. You curl up on your couch to watch television; some commercials catch your eye, while you pay no attention to others. We all know there's "good" marketing and "bad" marketing, but how do you determine what's truly "good"?

Here's some homework for you: Start paying closer attention to the marketing you see around you. Keep a pad of paper with you at all times, and jot down your thoughts as you see various marketing materials in stores, at airports, on websites, on Facebook pages, in magazines, or near bus stops — everywhere you see them. Which marketing techniques do you find good, and which ones do you think are not so great? What's working well for other brands, and what isn't working?

Maybe you like marketing that speaks directly to the customer in language that's easily understood, or maybe you like ads that are a little bit mysterious. You may respond to humor, a clear call to action, or an ad that evokes an emotion in you. What is compelling? What resonates? What makes you want to buy?

Get into a regular habit of assessing marketing. Every day, challenge yourself to review ten pieces of marketing you run across (once you start paying attention, you'll see many more than that — guaranteed). Pretty soon, you'll be able to clarify in your own mind what is good marketing and what is marketing that has missed its mark. You'll learn as much from bad marketing as from good.

In particular, pay special attention to brands that are trying to attract the same Target Market as yours. You can then use that information, along with the tips and techniques outlined in this book, to build your own brand. I call that "spitting out the bones" — keeping what works for you and throwing out what isn't useful.

Who is Responsible for Marketing in Your Organization?

Right now, picture the people in your company who are responsible for marketing your brand. Who comes to mind? Maybe you're thinking of one particular employee or a handful of staff members. They may even have the word "Marketing" in their job titles. Perhaps you're a solo-preneur, and you're thinking, "I'm the only one responsible."

Branding Myth:
Only people with "Marketing" in their titles are responsible for marketing.

Not true — consider that a branding myth "busted!" *Everyone* in your organization is responsible for marketing your brand, even if your company is small and/or you are a "one-man (or one-woman) show." In this book, we'll unleash the power that comes with recognizing how everybody you know is part of your marketing team and can, therefore, help you market your brand. And it doesn't have to cost you anything.

What's Holding You Back From Success?

Now that you know the differences between key branding terms, let's talk about the biggest single obstacle that holds all types of business owners back from successfully marketing their products and services. What do you think it is? You might say, "not enough money" or "not enough people" or "not enough time or resources." You might even think it's the economy. But none of these obstacles is as limiting a factor as the one I'm about to share with you.

What is that biggest obstacle? *A limiting mindset.* Yes, indeed, by focusing on what you *don't* have rather than focusing on what you *do* have, you are most likely to end up with a brand that's stuck and unable to grow. It's a bit like the glass-half-empty versus glass-half-full mindset. It's incredibly debilitating, and I've seen it cripple businesses all across the globe.

Do you occasionally fall prey to this limiting mindset? If so, here's an interesting and fun challenge to give that glass-half-empty mindset a run for its money.

The Wisdom of a Paperclip

Grab a pen and paper or sit down in front of your computer. Set the timer for three minutes, and within that timeframe, make a list of everything you can think of that you cannot do with a paperclip. That's right — what you *cannot* do with a paperclip.

Challenge yourself! When I do this exercise in my workshops, someone often says something like, "I cannot *eat* a paperclip!" And everyone nods their heads in agreement. But, of course, that isn't true. Think about it … you *could* absolutely eat a paperclip. Chop it up into little pieces and sprinkle it on your salad. It would be crazy, mind you, and might very well end in a trip to the emergency room. But the point is: You *can* eat a paperclip if you want.

Likewise, you might say, "You cannot *write* with a paperclip." Once again, I have to disagree. You could unfold a paperclip, dip it into some ink, and voilà! You've got a "paperclip pen."

Not long into this exercise, it becomes clear that you can do far more with a paperclip than you thought. In fact, try as they might, a lot of workshop attendees come up with absolutely nothing they truly *cannot* do with a paperclip.

Your "Marketing Mindset"

What's the point of that exercise? A limiting mindset may be the single biggest roadblock holding you back from building the thriving brand you want and deserve. Shifting your thinking from "I can't" to "I can" is one of the most accessible and powerful tools you have — and it doesn't cost you a penny.

This same mindset applies to reading this book. Throughout *Smarter Branding Without Breaking the Bank,* you will read about all sorts of marketing and branding examples from companies with different ownership structures and different sizes, from solo-preneurs to small, local, niche businesses, to medium-sized companies and large multi-national conglomerates. You'll read about service businesses, manufacturers, and product distributors. We'll look at business-to-business companies ("B2B") that sell to other companies, as well as business-to-consumer companies ("B2C") that sell directly to the end user.

As you look at those examples, you might find yourself falling into the "can't" trap. "That case study doesn't apply to my brand because we're too small," or "We're a service business operating in a niche area, so that example wouldn't work for us." If that happens, beware! Stop what you're doing, grab a paperclip, and help yourself shift back into the "can" mode of thinking. Just as there's more that you can do with a paperclip than you thought, there's more that you can do to market your brand than you probably ever dreamed imaginable. Indeed, throughout these chapters, I'm going to give you a loaded arsenal of marketing examples, ideas, strategies, and possibilities that won't require mega-bucks or lots of time, and almost all of these ideas can be applied across the board.

Make a concerted effort to shift your thinking away from "that example doesn't apply to my brand" to "how could that example apply to my brand?" If you do, you'll be amazed to discover how many more ideas you have at your fingertips than you ever realized.

Staying Open 24/7

To serve as a constant reminder, do what I do and keep a foot-long paperclip at your desk![2] Don't have space for that size of paperclip? Then, put a normal-sized one in your pocket, by your computer, or wherever else you can see it on a regular basis. Let it serve as a constant reminder to hold on to that "marketing mindset." It will help you remember what you *can* do to build your brand instead of what you *cannot* do.

---

2. I buy my foot-long giant paperclips from a company call Great Big Stuff at www.GreatBigStuff.com. Check them out!

2

Don't Just Sit There on Your Assets

The Five Brand-Building Resources You Already Have

"If you count all your assets, you always show a profit."
— Robert Quillen, 20th-century American journalist

A s I've mentioned before, you have many low-cost or no-cost marketing resources right at your fingertips. In fact, there are five major assets I guarantee you already have, and you can leverage all of them immediately to build your brand and grow your business. Those five assets are what this book is all about. They are powerful but also incredibly simple, and that's what makes them work.

Throughout these chapters, we'll dive deep into each of the five assets in great detail, and you'll understand them better as we go along. But let's outline them briefly here so that you can get an understanding of what's coming.

Asset #1: *Your Brand Positioning.* You will craft a unique and distinctive positioning for your brand in the marketplace. This is fundamental and will serve as the foundation for everything you will do in relation to growing your brand. In fact, this subject is so important that we will focus on it for the next several chapters.

Asset #2: *Your Customers.* Without customers, you don't have a business, so you already know how important they are. What you might not know, though, is how your customers can be a free-flowing fountain of ideas and support to help you brand your business more effectively.

Asset #3:   *Your Products and Services.* You already have these, as well. Using them to build a brand is a matter of turning them into a point of superiority ... even if you don't think they're superior right now. We'll share lots of ways to make your products or services stand out in the market.

Asset #4:   *Your Team.* Even if you believe your "brand-building team" is very small, I guarantee you that it's a lot bigger than you think. We'll talk about how to define, build, and leverage a mega-team of people to increase the power of your brand.

Asset #5:   *Your Competitors.* You may be asking yourself, "How can my competitors help build my brand?" I think you'll be pleasantly surprised to discover how much competitors really *can* help ... and they'll have no idea they're doing it.

I hope you can see that you do indeed already have these five assets. You just may not yet appreciate how each of these can serve to grow your brand into the kind that keeps customers coming back for more.

Are you ready? Let's dive right into Asset #1.

3

A GPS for Your Brand

An Introduction to Brand-Building Asset #1 — Positioning

"Is Google a 'better' search engine? Is Red Bull a 'better' energy drink? Is Microsoft a 'better' operating system? Or did these companies just build better brands?"

— Laura Ries, Media Commentator

THE #1 MOST IMPORTANT, low-cost asset you already have in your brand-building arsenal is your "brand positioning." We'll explore what brand positioning is and why I think this asset is so fundamental but, for now, think of your positioning as the "GPS for your brand." Without positioning, your brand is like a boat adrift in the water with no place to go and no wind beneath its sails.

Positioning is absolutely fundamental to the success of any brand, yours included. In fact, positioning is so important that we're going to spend the next few chapters focusing on it before we get to Brand Building Asset #2.

So, what is this all-important asset?

Brand positioning is the way you want your customers to **perceive, think,** *and* **feel** *about your brand versus competition.*

Notice that I highlighted three words in this definition: *perceive, think,* and *feel.* Let's start with the first one.

Perception

Perception is reality in marketing. It means that how your brand is viewed in the marketplace *is* what your brand stands for, whether you like it or not.

In fact, I sometimes work with company leaders who say, "We want to find out what our brand stands for." So, we'll go out and hire a market research agency to uncover what the company's customers think of its brand. The results come in, and I can't tell you how many times I've sat in a meeting with the company's owner to review the research agency's report, only to have the following scenario take place: The company leader sits there, thumbing through the pages, and his or her face switches from hope and anticipation to a frown and a scowl, followed by: "No … this can't be right. That isn't what our brand stands for!" But, of course, it *is* how their customers perceive their brand, whether they like the results or not.

So, once again, perception in marketing is reality … and it can sometimes be a harsh one. The key is: If you don't like the way your brand is perceived, it's up to you to take charge and change it. That's where brand positioning comes into play.

Thinking and Feeling

The second and third highlighted words in the definition of brand positioning are also critical. We make brand choices based both on how we *think* and *feel* about them.

The most successful brand builders have a very clear understanding of the way they want customers to think and feel about their brands. They know they need to grab the minds of their customers, as well as their hearts.

Here's a "true confession" from my own life: I've been using the same brand of toothpaste for 20 years! When I first started using that particular brand, it was a *rational* choice because the toothpaste served the important purpose of helping me to prevent cavities. So I "thought" rationally about that purchase decision.

But don't think for a minute that I've stayed loyal to that same brand for 20 years based solely on a rational decision! No, that brand has reached out over the years and made an emotional connection with me that goes far beyond anything rational or functional. I'm loyal to this particular toothpaste brand because...well, honestly, I have a *relationship* with the brand. I trust it. So, there is a definite feeling involved in my choice of toothpaste. I guarantee you there are probably better performing toothpaste brands out there right now, but I don't care.

Can you see now that how your customers think and feel about your brand can lead to long-term loyalty and an increase in revenues?

The bottom line is: If you don't take the time to create your positioning consciously, your customers might be perceiving, thinking, and feeling about your brand in ways you don't want. That will put you on a straight and narrow path to failure.

A Few Brand Positioning Myths Debunked

Whenever I talk about brand positioning to a solo-preneur or a group of small-to-medium business owners, several branding myths rise to the surface. Here's one example:

Branding Myth:
"You say we have a positioning, but we really don't.
After all, we've never written one down."

A branding myth busted! Why? Here's the reality: Whether you've written down your positioning or not, your brand has one.

Remember: Brand positioning is how your customers perceive, think, and feel about your brand. So, just by virtue of the fact that your customers know of your brand, their perceptions, thoughts, and feelings are happening right this minute. In other words, you may think your brand stands for reliability, but if your customers don't think so, it really doesn't matter what you think.

Let's try a personal example to bring this to light.

- Stop for a moment and think about your very favorite brand. Picture it in your mind. Examine the perceptions, thoughts, and feelings you have about this brand.

- Now, think about a brand you dislike. You have a particular set of perceptions, thoughts, and feelings about this brand, too. You can bet that your perception of the negative brand isn't what the brand's company *wants* you to think or feel. Yet, your perceptions, thoughts, and feelings about this brand are preventing you from buying it.

I hope you can see by now that you not only already have a brand positioning but that it is alive and kicking and making a big impact on your success or failure.

"But We're Small!"

Are you a solo-preneur or in charge of a smaller-sized operation? If you're like a lot of people I know who fit into this category, you may have bought into yet another misconception.

Branding Myth:
"But my company is small — so we don't really need a brand positioning."

Again, myth busted! Nothing could be further from the truth. In fact, smaller companies need positioning *even more* than big companies. Let's face it: A big conglomerate can afford to get it wrong over and over. They have the funds to begin again if something doesn't work. Small businesses, on the other hand, usually have fewer resources — fewer people, less money, and less time — so even small marketing and branding mistakes can cost a lot. These smaller businesses can't afford to be unclear about their positioning. If their positioning is vague, it could mean the end of their business — fast.

"But We're a B2B Company!"

Another objection about positioning that I often hear is from business-to-business companies. They say, "Give us a break, Brenda — you spent years marketing consumer goods directly to end users. *That's* where brand positioning really matters."

Branding Myth:
"Brand positioning is only for consumer goods companies."

Once again, dead wrong. Positioning is fundamental to the success of *any* type of business. In B2B companies in particular, customers often think "parts is parts," so crafting a unique positioning is your chance to truly differentiate yourself from your competition.

Positioning allows any company — B2Bs included — to find that special "sweet spot" in the marketplace that they, and they alone, can own. Your positioning helps you hone in on what is unique about your brand. If you find yourself constantly pressured to compete based primarily on price, positioning can be your ticket off of that never-ending, self-defeating hamster wheel.

Business-to-business company margins are typically smaller, too, so there is usually less money to spend on marketing and branding. That's why a laser-focused brand positioning makes your communications even more effective and targeted. The outcome? You get more bang for your buck, and your brand grows in the process.

Great Brands Don't Get to Be Great By Accident

Indeed, great brands become great because the marketers in charge of those brands determine right up front how they want their brands to be perceived. They define their positioning clearly and set out to communicate that positioning to their customers via everything they do — day in and day out.

Based on my own experience, I estimate that about 80% of SMEs haven't taken charge of their brand positioning. They leave it to chance, which means their customers end up with wrong or negative perceptions of their brands.

How about you? What is *your* brand positioning? One thing is for sure: If *you* aren't exactly clear what your brand stands for, you can be sure your customers aren't clear about it either. Or, even worse: If you don't take charge of your brand's positioning, your competition will! They will position their own brands until yours has fallen right to the bottom — or until it's out of the market. Without a clear positioning, you are simply not in the driver's seat, and your competition will decide for you what your brand stands for. So, it's your job to decide who you are and to communicate that to your customers.

You may be thinking: "If my brand positioning exists in the minds of my customers, what can I do to change those perceptions, thoughts, and feelings? How can I establish an emotional connection with them?" There's a lot you can do, and the next several chapters will show you just that.

Crafting and understanding your positioning may not be the easiest of tasks, but as you read through the next few chapters, you will learn exactly how to create a customized Positioning Statement for your own brand. We will go through it line by line until you feel comfortable with it. That's how you ensure your brand positioning is what you want it to be. That's how you affect the perceptions, thoughts, and feelings of your current and potential customers. And if you do this, I guarantee you'll be ahead of 80% of the brands and businesses out there.

Your Brand Positioning Statement

The best way to create a powerful positioning is to adopt a tried-and-true framework — the same one that has been used successfully for years by the most powerful brands in the world. This framework is in the form of a "Brand Positioning Statement" that clearly articulates exactly what you want your brand to stand for. This statement then serves as an all-important brand GPS — kind of like your North Star — so that you'll always know where you need to go with your brand. With this statement in hand, you will also know how to communicate your positioning to your customers to more effectively build your business.

The Six Elements of Your Brand Positioning Statement

Stop for a moment and think again about your favorite brand that we mentioned earlier. Got it in your head? Now, here's a secret about that brand that very few people know: That brand's positioning is made up of six elements.

How do I know? Well, *every* brand's positioning consists of six elements — yours included!

These six elements all work together like a piston engine. The success of every brand depends a great deal on how well the marketers managing those six elements are clear on what they stand for and how to use them. In fact, how well those six elements are managed makes the difference between a mediocre brand, a good brand, and a brand that becomes a thriving, revenue-producing household name. It's the same for your brand.

So, what are these six elements that will determine whether your brand wins or loses in the marketplace?

1. *Target Group.* Who is going to buy your brand? Men, women, college graduates, people with high incomes, people with low incomes? What are the dreams and fears of these people? What attitudes do they have toward the type of product or service you sell? What can you tell about them by the way they act toward a particular brand?

2. *Needs.* What does your Target Group need? When a company creates a brand, it tries to respond to a Need in the marketplace that is new or that hasn't been filled as well as it could.

3. *Competitive Framework.* What similar brands in the marketplace might your customer choose over your brand? These brands make up your Competitive Framework. Many brands compete for your business. Why do you choose one over another?

These first three listed above are what I call "outside" elements. That's because they have to do with characteristics that are outside of your brand itself: your Target Group, the Needs of your Target Group, and your competitive set of brands.

The last three are what I consider "inside" elements because they are all integral parts of your brand: the Benefits your brand offers, the Reasons Why your customers should believe in your Benefits, and the Character of your brand.

4. *Benefits.* What does your brand offer its customers? Your toothpaste brand, for example, may prevent your children from getting cavities and make you feel like a great parent. These are the Benefits it offers you.

5. *Reasons Why.* Why should your Target Group believe that your brand can deliver the Benefits you say it can? A particular ingredient, for example, may prove that your toothpaste can fight cavities.

6. *Brand Character.* This is the "personality" of your brand — its demeanor, disposition, and overriding attitude. What words would you use to describe your brand if that brand were a person? Mercedes Benz and Ferrari are both luxury car brands, but the Brand Characters of the two are quite different.

These six elements all work together to carve out the specific place in the market you want your brand to own. It's your unique piece of "mental real estate" in your customer's mind.

Differentiate, Differentiate, Differentiate! Product Brand Examples

Even if you find yourself in a very competitive playing field, not to worry! To illustrate how brand positioning can differentiate product brands from one another, let's consider the chewing gum market.

- **Hubba Bubba** is a brand for bubble gum lovers that provides big bubble-blowing satisfaction.

- **Clorets** is a gum that helps eliminate bad breath.

- **Dentyne Fire and Ice** offers intense flavor.

- The **Five** brand of gum is sugar-free and targets more health-conscious consumers. It also appeals to customers who want to attract the opposite sex.

- **Orbit** provides white and beautiful teeth. They say, "You can have beautiful teeth even if the rest of you isn't so beautiful."

You can see how each of these chewing gum brands is working hard to own a specific — and differentiated — piece of real estate in the minds of chewing gum consumers.

Differentiate, Differentiate, Differentiate! Service Brand Examples

What if your business offers a service rather than product? The same concept applies.

Let's compare personal trainers to get an idea of how to set yourself apart in a service industry. Just a quick glance through the Internet reveals a number of personal trainers who have each found a specific niche to own in a very competitive market.

- First, consider Marv — a fitness trainer who calls himself the fitness guru "for the urban warrior." He focuses on outdoor fitness in a boot-camp type of atmosphere.

- Another personal trainer says she focuses on the combination of both mind wellness and body wellness — a different kind of brand positioning to own.

- Yet another personal trainer I found specializes in working only with women, honing in on women's issues and women-specific physical health needs.

- Then there's Michael George, who positions himself as "trainer to the stars" — quite a unique (and intriguing) place to own in the market.

- Last is a trainer who differentiates himself by going to people's homes and training specifically in the sport of basketball.

Each of these trainers is uniquely differentiated in the market, and their clear brand positionings are what make them distinctive.

Do You Know What You *Aren't?*

As you determine what you want your brand to stand for in the marketplace, it's equally important to decide what you *don't* want to stand for. To illustrate this, let me share a personal story.

When I decided to start my own business after so many years in big corporations, I admit it: I was terrified! I didn't know where my first customers would come from, but I *did* know that I wanted to focus my new business on my passions: branding and marketing. During my very first week of running the business, I received a phone call from an executive at a large local company who said, "We hear you're starting a new business, so we're hoping you could come in and train our Sales team on some good sales strategies."

Sales?? Drats!

I was shaking in my shoes, but I took a deep breath and said, "No, thank you." After all, Sales wasn't what I wanted my brand to stand for. I wanted to own the branding and marketing space. But I will tell you honestly: Turning down that very first offer was hard! Nevertheless, I knew I had to keep my brand positioning "GPS" on track, and that meant only accepting assignments in branding and marketing.

Exactly two days later — I kid you not — I received another phone call from another large company. They said, "We hear you've started your own business, and we'd love for you to come in and conduct some training on a human resources topic." Once again, I took a deep breath and said, "No." By this point in time, I really felt as though the universe was testing me! You can imagine how nerve-racking it was to turn down yet another assignment. But I had to if I was to stay true to my desired brand. Fortunately, the very next day, a phone call came in from someone who offered me my first marketing engagement, and I've been working happily in branding and marketing ever since.

Could I have done those presentations on Sales and HR? Sure, probably. And could I have used the revenue? Absolutely! But saying "yes" to those engagements would have left potential customers confused as to what I stood for.

The moral of the story? Be true to what you really want your brand to stand for, know what that is, and have the courage to stick to that positioning — and say "no" when it makes sense.

The Positioning Wheel — The Center of It All

Here is a visual of what I call the "Positioning Wheel." It gives you a good idea of how the six elements work together to drive everything you do with your business.

The six elements of your brand positioning fit in the middle of the wheel, and every aspect of your business is influenced by that positioning.

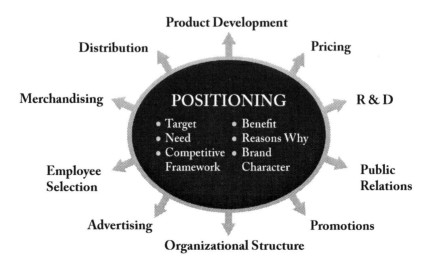

To demonstrate how this works, let's pretend you've decided to open a fitness center. You've researched the market and determined that your potential customers are people who want to be able to exercise at any time of the day. So, you'll have to keep your center open 24/7 to respond to that Need. It also means you will need to hire enough staff for three shifts, round the clock. You can already see how your positioning will impact your operating system and your human resources policies.

This particular customer target also desires the very best exercise equipment, so your positioning will drive your capital expenditures. After all, you're going to have to purchase and maintain state-of-the-art exercise machines. This, in turn, means that you'll want to hire excellent personal trainers who will know how to run and operate the equipment. Once again, this affects your human resources/hiring policies.

Your Target Group wants a luxury experience, so that will require you to install very nice changing rooms, steam rooms, saunas, massage services, and more. This lets you know how much money you will need to spend to address those Needs and be successful in your market. As a result, you know immediately that you'll have to charge a higher price for your fitness center in order to cover the costs of your top-notch facility. So, your positioning also drives your pricing policies.

Lastly, you'll want to get the word out about your new fitness center to your Target Group, which means you'll need to concentrate your marketing efforts in places that can reach this high-end, more discerning clientele. So, your positioning also affects your marketing strategy, as you make sure your efforts reach your specific Target Group.

As you can see, all six elements of a brand positioning — in fact, every single word you choose to put in your Positioning Statement — will impact what you and your team need to do to build your brand. It's that important.

Let's get started creating your own unique Positioning Statement — the first step toward creating a brand that will capture the hearts and minds of your customers.

4

THE POWER OF A BULL'S EYE

Core Positioning Element #1 — Target Group Overview

"It's about the audience. It always has been."
— KATE SMITH, SINGER

THE FIRST ELEMENT in your Brand Positioning Statement is your Target Group — the people who are most likely to be interested in your brand. Think of it as the group of people who will ultimately buy your products or services.

The key to success in choosing a Target Group is that their Needs and concerns should be similar, and the more specific you are, the better. That means making choices, which is often the hardest part of developing your brand positioning. As author Peter Drucker said, "Wherever you see a successful business, someone once made a courageous decision." Choosing your Target Group is one of those courageous decisions.

Often, when I ask entrepreneurs to describe their Target Group, they tell me that their product or service is for "everyone" or for some extremely large group of people like "adults" or "all women." They tell me that no one is *outside* their Target Group. But one of the most important lessons of branding is — and I hope you're really paying attention here — **your brand cannot be all things to all people.** No brand is successful at targeting everyone. *No brand.*

Okay, well, there may be *certain* brands that are so large and iconic and have such mass appeal that they come *close* to being for everyone — like Coke, for example. But let's be honest — would you give Coke to a six-month-old? No, so it still isn't for absolutely "everyone."

Even if your brand *is* targeted toward a large market, that's a risk. Why? Well, let's continue looking at Coke. What did its biggest competitor do to find its own market in which to play? If you review Pepsi's advertising, you'll see that Pepsi chose to focus on a Target Group that is far more specific than Coke's. In fact, the marketers at Pepsi were downright clever. They knew that Coke was trying to be everything to everybody, so they carved out their own area in the market in order to differentiate their brand from Coke.

Pepsi focused on a Target Group of young people — the "new generation" — and people who "think young." This worked great for them — after all, who doesn't want to be considered a "young thinker"? This was enough to create a powerful difference between these two brand giants, despite the fact that they have very similar products. So, the key to success in choosing your Target Group is to make tough choices about who *is* in your Target Group and who is *not*.

Choosing Your "In" Crowd

How do you make wise choices about your Target Group? How do you go about deciding who's in and who's out? The easiest place to start — and a trap that a lot of marketers fall into — is by only defining your Target Group in a very "provable" way. For example, you might say, "women between the ages of 20 and 35 who make $35,000 or more per year and live in cities." That sounds reasonable, right? Let's test it out.

- Picture in your mind a woman of about 30 sitting on a city park bench. She's taking her lunch break, and she's dressed in a black suit jacket and skirt with a white blouse buttoned up to her neck, panty hose, and short black heels. Her hair is up in a bun, she wears glasses, and she's working on her laptop. Do you have that visual in your mind?

- Now, compare that image with this one: Envision a woman in her mid-20s walking down the street in an urban area. She's dressed in brightly colored, trendy, hip-hop-inspired clothes — name-brand jeans, suspenders, a t-shirt with some bling, and a diamond nose ring.

Do both of those women fit the defined target of "women between the ages of 20 and 35 who make $35,000 or more a year and live in cities?" It's possible! The question is: Are these two women likely to want the same products or services? Are they likely to have the same Needs? Probably not. This shows you how limiting "provable facts" like age, location, and income can be when it comes to defining your Target Group. Good, true branders go beyond just these simple "demographics."

Don't Just Scratch the Surface — Dig Deep!

As you can tell from the example above, "demographics" are provable facts about people — aspects such as age, gender, income, education, location, nationality, etc. It's the kind of information you would be asked to supply on a census information form.

But demographics are just the tip of the iceberg when it comes to getting to know your Target Group. You need to go beyond that. Think about it: If all you knew about someone was how old they were, how much money they made, and where they lived, you really wouldn't know much about that person. You would have only scratched the surface of who that person is. I hope you can see how focusing only on demographics can seriously limit your ability to build a powerful brand.

Please don't get me wrong. You definitely need to know "some" demographics, but smart branders go far beyond the simple provable facts, digging deep to get a much better understanding of their Target Group. You want to go below the surface and find out what truly makes these people tick.

The bottom line is this: The better you know your Target Group, the better you will know how to market to them effectively. And that's fundamental to building a powerhouse brand.

Brands That Excel at Target Practice

Let's take a look at a few other brands that have carefully defined Target Groups. We've talked about Pepsi and its focus on "people who think young." Another brand that has done a great job of focusing on a specific Target Group is Apple.

Apple focuses on creative people who think differently, and everything they do is targeted to that "mindset." This intense focus on the customer's way of thinking has served Apple so well that, during a recent recession, the company grew by double digits at a time when other brands were *losing* business in the double digits! This consistent focus on catering to the Needs of a creative audience led Apple to develop the Mac Mini, the iPod Shuffle, iTunes, iPhone, iPad, and on and on. And, most importantly, this intense Target Group focus differentiates the company a great deal from Microsoft, its biggest competitor.

Now, I recognize that Coca-Cola, Pepsi, and Apple are all enormous corporations. So, you may be saying, "But, Brenda, those are big companies! I'm just starting out — how I can afford *not* to be all things to all people?"

Here's the surprising truth: The smaller you are, the more targeted you need to be. It may sound counter-intuitive, but if you don't focus, you will most likely get lost in the shuffle of your competition. Why? Because you'll be trying to stretch your limited resources to please all masters. Focusing on a specific target is the key to success.

Let me share a few more examples of companies who have done well by carefully defining their Target Groups. Consider a small company named Groovy Maps that began in Asia and now sells its maps all over the world. Groovy Maps was trying to compete with other map makers by targeting "all tourists." But, while doing some customer research, they uncovered a smaller Target Market of business people who only came into large Asian cities for about three days. They spent those days in business meetings but, come nightfall, these same people were ready to get out and have some fun.

So, Groovy Maps got to work and created a specific map for this group of people. The map not only included the essentials for the daytime work crowd — a subway map, how and where to catch cabs, and where key office buildings and hotels were located — but also included where to find the best night spots. The company was so successful with this concept that it expanded across Asia and Australia. Now, its maps are sold all over the world via Amazon.com and elsewhere.

Here are some more examples:

- Waste Management Siam is a company that identified and successfully focused its Target on a particular corporate mindset — environmentally-conscious companies — long before being green was popular.

- Maybank is a bank that specifically targets Muslims who follow Islamic law. This is a very important — and often unmet — Need, since Islamic law prohibits certain payments or acceptance of interest fees for loaning money.

- Hay House is a publishing company founded by Louise Hay, the author of the book *You Can Heal Your Life*. It targets readers who have a particular mindset: They are passionate about spiritual and personal development.

- W Hotels targets people who are trendsetters. When it comes to choosing a hotel, they want to attract those who are interested in the latest, the newest, and the hippest. According to a quote from their global brand leader, W Hotels' overall intention is to be "the coolest place in town."

So, as you can see, bull's eye focus is essential to building a successful brand. Once you know who you're marketing to, you can more clearly determine *how* to market to them.

5

DRAW YOUR BOW AND POINT YOUR ARROW
Core Positioning Element #1 — Target Group Application

*"Getting to know someone else involves curiosity about
where they have come from, who they are."*
— PENELOPE LIVELY, FICTION AUTHOR

HOW DO YOU DEFINE your Target Group so that you can dig deeper
and really "know" who they are? In many ways, it's simple: There
are six parts to deeply understanding your Target Group:

1. Demographics

2. Psychographics

3. Motivations/Attitudes

4. Current Usage

5. Behaviors

6. Needs

Let's dive into each, using the 24/7 fitness center example from
Chapter 3 to demonstrate how they work.

1. **Demographics.** We covered demographics in the last chapter.
   Remember: They're important — no question — but they're only
   the start of your Target Group definition. Unfortunately, too many
   marketers start and stop with demographics, never investigating
   further to learn more about the people who make up their Target
   Group.

Applying demographics to the 24/7 fitness center, we could say that the demographics are "men and women between the ages of 30 and 50 who live or work within five miles of the center, have extremely tight schedules, and have household incomes of more than $100,000." If you look at each part of this demographic definition, you'll see that I could "prove" each one.

2. **Psychographics.** As mentioned in the last chapter, this is a critical component that involves going deeper into the mindset of the Target Group. It's about putting a label on the group to help you describe them. For our 24/7 fitness center example, the Psychographic might be "round-the-clock exercise experience elitists." They are "elite" in their thinking and looking for a powerful and positive exercise "experience," no matter the time of day.

3. **Motivations and Attitudes.** This applies to the motivations and attitudes of your Target Group toward your particular product or service category, so it's important to be very specific.

   For our fitness center example, the Target Group is motivated by an exercise environment where they can be around people of a similar social status. They see exercise as a privilege and an enjoyable experience to be carried out at any time that's convenient for them. Another constraint on their time — like a fitness center with specific open and close times — is simply unacceptable. After a hard workout, they want to pamper themselves with an on-site massage or sauna because they like the idea of relaxing and getting away from the pressures of home and work. For them, no exercise at all is better than a bad exercise experience.

4, 5. **Current Usage,** and **Behaviors.** Numbers 4 and 5 work together and, again, it's important to keep in mind that this covers usages and behaviors with regard to the product or service category in question. What does your Target Group currently use to meet their needs? If they aren't using your brand, what brand are they using? Or, are they not yet using any company's products or services in your category?

Again, using the 24/7 fitness center as our model, we might say that the current usage and behavior of this Target Group involves popping in and out of different high-end gyms, trying to find one that suits them best. They also visit different five-star spas, trying various massages and treatments. But not one particular place fits all of their Needs. This group is discerning, so you could imagine someone in this Target Group walking into a gym and, just as quickly, turning around and walking right back out if they don't feel the gym fits their exceptionally high standards.

6. **Needs.** If you've completed all of the above five Target Group elements well, those five elements should very naturally lead toward this sixth, and last, component. Needs are actually the second positioning element, and they are so important that we're going to explore them in greater detail in the next chapter. But suffice it to say that knowing very clearly what your Target Group needs is one of the most fundamental ingredients to the success of your brand.

Making the Pieces Fit

Once you're clear on all six of these individual parts, it's time to put them together. Like a jigsaw puzzle, each piece fills a specific role to create the total picture. Let's take the Snickers candy bar brand as an example. In my extensive international travels, I've not yet visited a country where Snickers *doesn't* have a presence! It's a powerful, global brand.

The example here is "inferred," which means it's been pulled together based on what it "seems" the six components of the Snickers brand's Target Group would be. In fact, this example comes to us thanks to Richard Czerniawski and Michael Maloney of Brand Development Network International (BDNI), who regularly work with multinational brands to help them develop their Positioning Statements. Richard and Mike came up with this definition after carefully reviewing the Snickers brand's television and print advertisements, promotions, website, in-store communications, packaging, etc. Let's take a look.

Snickers Target Group:

"Tied up" adults and teens whose daily routines find them confined for long periods of time in office meetings, at school, or on an airplane. They typically snack between meals on chips, cookies, nuts, and a variety of candy bars and other types of bars. They feel that they deserve a tasty treat indulgence during these confined times.

Let's dissect this description to look at each individual component of the Snickers Target Group:

- **Demographics**: *Adults and teens whose daily routines find them confined for long periods of time in office meetings, at school, or on an airplane.* Note that all of this is information you can prove.

- **Psychographics:** These adults and teens are *"tied up."* If you think about it, being "tied up" is not just a provable fact, but it also reflects a *mindset* of feeling trapped in a meeting, a classroom, an airplane, etc.

- **Behaviors**: *They typically snack between meals.* This is a "telling" behavior because you can see it.

- **Current Usages:** *They usually snack on chips, cookies, nuts, and a variety of candy bars and other types of bars.* This tells us what competitive products Snickers consumers are using now, as well as what they aren't using.

- **Motivations and Attitudes:** *They feel that they deserve a tasty treat indulgence during these confined times.* This helps us understand the Snickers' customers' attitudes about the candy bar category.

(We'll talk about the sixth element of the Snickers' Target Group — Needs — in the next chapter.)

Do you see how all five of these pieces fit together like a puzzle to define who Snickers is targeting? Now, let's apply these components to your own brand.

Who is Your "Target of One"?

Even with these Target Group components laid out clearly, you may be feeling a bit overwhelmed by the thought of defining your own brand's target. Many business owners feel that way at first. Luckily, there's a great tool you can use that I like to call the "Target of One." This allows you to focus on *one* person (or *one* company if yours is a B2B company) — one specific customer who has the characteristics of your Target Group. You might create a profile of this individual by thinking of your very best customer/client — current or past — and describing that individual in detail.

If you haven't yet started your business, this person or company would be your vision of your best customer in the future — sort of your "dream customer." Would it be a specific individual? A big company or a small company? What is this individual's or company's attitude toward the kind of brand you want to build? How does this individual or company feel about the types of products or services you offer?

No matter how you define this Target of One, it should be the type of customer whose Needs you can meet spot on. It should be a customer with high potential to remain loyal to your brand. This person, or the key decision-maker within a company in the case of a business-to-business client, will be extremely happy with the value received from your brand.

The exciting thing about this approach is that it works equally well for small companies and solo-preneurs as it does for multi-billion dollar brands. Even huge conglomerates have to work locally by replicating their Target of One 500,000 times. This is a powerful concept because the more you focus on this perfect target, the more you will draw perfect customers to you. The key is to make your target as real as possible and really bring it to life.

American Advertising Hall of Famer, Morris Hite, put it this way: "There is no such thing as national advertising. All advertising is local and personal. It's one man or woman reading one newspaper in the kitchen or watching TV in the den." In today's digital age — taking into account the "back-and-forth" of social media — this is even more true. So, it doesn't matter if your company is small or large; you still have to focus on the personal side of your Target Group and think of them as individuals.

Ask and Ye Shall Receive

Asking yourself useful questions about your Target Group and Target of One can be a helpful way of defining your customers. Here are just a few questions to get you started:

Demographic Information

(Provable social characteristics, such as age, sex, income, and education)

- Name
- Age
- Marital status
- Number of children
- Income
- Nationality
- Where do they live (city or rural area)?
- What kind of school did they attend?
- What's the highest level of education they achieved?
- Are they living where they grew up, or did they move to a new area?
- Where have they traveled?
- What is the nature of their business/work?
- How long have they been working in their current job?
- Did they switch careers at some point?

What other demographic-related questions can you think of for your Target of One?

Psychographic Information

(More psychologically-oriented personality traits of this person, including attitudes, mindset, etc.)

- What are their priorities in life?
- What matters most to them?
- Where does family fit into their priorities?

- What role does career play in their lives?
- How and why did they choose their current career?
- How satisfied are they now?
- What dreams do they have?
- Do they aspire to something more in life?
- What are their hobbies and interests?
- How do they spend their spare time?
- What are their favorite foods, music, sports?
- Who is their personal hero?
- What are their hopes and fears?

What other psychographic-related questions can you think of for your Target of One?

Another thing you can do to get a better handle on your Target Group is to grab some magazines and look for pictures of people who you believe would "fit" into your Target Group. For example, the 24/7 fitness center might choose a photo of a reasonably fit man sitting behind a nice desk in a corner office dressed in an expensive business suit. Snickers might choose a picture of a teenager sitting in a classroom, looking a bit bored. If your Target Group is relaxed, fun, and casual — perhaps even romantic — an image of a guy playing a guitar while his girlfriend rests her head on his shoulder might work for you. Having a visual representation of your Target of One can help clarify and bring to life who your customers are. And once you know who they really are, you're well on your way to creating a successful brand.

6

MEET THEIR NEEDS AND YOU'LL SUCCEED

Core Positioning Element #2 — Customer Needs

"Before you build a better mousetrap, it helps to know
if there are any mice out there."

— YOGI BERRA, PROFESSIONAL BASEBALL PLAYER
AND COACH

YOGI BERRA KNEW what he was talking about. If no one needs the "better mousetrap" you've developed, you won't have a successful brand — pure and simple. You'll just end up with a warehouse full of mousetraps.

So, the next step is to take the definition of your Target Group and determine what they *need*. This is a truly fundamental part of your Positioning Statement, and everything else that makes your brand positioning a success will follow from this Core Positioning Element #2.

Customer Needs can be defined in three different ways:

- A problem that requires a solution,

- A problem that is not currently being addressed well enough in the marketplace,

   and/or

- A new problem that your customer doesn't even know exists.

Let's look at examples of brands in the marketplace that have filled each of these different types of Needs. When Crest toothpaste was first launched in the United States after World War II, it responded to the Need for better cavity protection, and that's how the marketers differentiated the Crest brand from other toothpastes. Like the proverbial better mousetrap, Gillette developed a razor that provided a closer shave, and IKEA provided quality furniture at an affordable price.

Viagra is a brand that fixed a problem that was not being addressed in the marketplace. It was the first prescription drug that responded to the Need for erectile dysfunction treatment. But then, Levitra did Viagra one better by providing erections for a full 24 hours. Cialis then came along with its own version of erectile dysfunction medication that lasted for 36 hours (!), causing the drug to be dubbed "the weekender." How's *that* for a better mousetrap?

What about a new problem that the customer doesn't even know exists? Apple has done a great job of filling this type of Need with its iPod brand. I mean, who knew we needed to carry around a small device that holds thousands of songs and videos? Apple knew it long before we did, and the iPod was born. In fact, today, carrying around an iPod has indeed become a genuine *Need* of a lot of people, but a few years ago, no one even knew what it was. The iPhone and the iPad are other examples of how Apple has discovered Needs that customers didn't even know they had.

Function and Emotion

If you remember anything about Needs, remember this: There are two types — functional and emotional — and the best brands address both.

- **Functional Needs** can be something physical or related to the body, such as a Need to quench your thirst or smooth wrinkles. Or the Need may be tangible, such as a Need for a smaller, lighter digital camera or an accurate tax return.

- **Emotional Needs**, as you can imagine, have to do with emotions, such as feeling proud as a parent because you're protecting your children's teeth from cavities. It could also refer to the peace of mind you feel from buying life insurance.

Too many brands focus only on the functional Needs, but when your brand fills an emotional Need, you establish a stronger connection with your Target Group, driving brand loyalty — the same kind of loyalty I've had for my toothpaste for 20 years. So, don't make the mistake a lot of marketers do and focus only on functional Needs. If you do, your competition will come along and lure your existing customers away by meeting an emotional Need. Don't let that happen to you!

In fact, Viagra is a great example of how filling an emotional Need helped beat the competition. You've definitely heard of Viagra, but you might not have heard about Viagra's competitors that I mentioned earlier, Levitra or Cialis. Why is that? Because Levitra and Cialis focused primarily on functional Needs, while Viagra's marketers were careful to also focus on emotional Needs. They made sure their customers knew that the product would help men restore their natural wholeness and establish the kinds of relationships they wanted. That's a powerful emotional Need and the key reason why Viagra has been more successful.

Let's take a look at some other popular brands.

- **Crest Toothpaste**
  Functional Need: Protection against cavities.
  Emotional Need: Relief knowing that your next visit to the dentist won't involve painful scraping and drilling.

- **Enfamil Infant Formula**
  Functional Need: Promoting your baby's brain development.
  Emotional Need: Confidence that you're doing the best you can for your child's future.

- **American Express Card**
  Functional Need: Financial flexibility to purchase what you want,when you want it.
  Emotional Need: Pride that you're using a credit card that reflects your level of financial success.

What about service businesses?

- **The accounting firm of Watts & Hershberger**
  Functional Need: Accuracy in tax preparation services.
  Emotional Need: Peace of mind knowing that your taxes are in good hands and you won't have to pay more taxes than absolutely necessary.

- **Four Seasons Hotels**
  Functional Need: A luxurious place to stay while on vacation that provides five-star service.

  Emotional Need: Pride in staying at one of the world's most prestigious hotels.

Uncovering the Emotional Needs of Your Target Group

Business owners often tell me that it's easy to uncover functional Needs, but they find it much more difficult to determine their Target Group's emotional Needs. If it's hard for you, too, concentrate on understanding how your Target of One *feels* — especially when using your brand or a competitor's brand. Remember that emotional Needs are all about feelings. In the examples given, notice the words used: relief, confidence, pride, and peace of mind.

Of course, another way to uncover emotional Needs is to pay attention to customer feedback. Listen to how customers express their feelings. They may say things like, "I was very satisfied with your product," "I was thrilled to finally find a service that could take care of this for me," "I'm really frustrated with the outcome," or "I'm angry that you didn't take care of this." Those are all clues to emotional Needs that can be uncovered and tapped.

My favorite example of a brand that uncovered an emotional Need is Howard Schultz and Starbucks. In the beginning, Starbucks was just a small coffee roasting company in Seattle, and Schultz was its Marketing Director. The company sent Schultz to Milan, Italy, to investigate a new roasting machine that was supposed to make a better-tasting cup of coffee, but he discovered much more while he was there.

When he arrived in Milan, he was told that the new roasting machine was being used in a number of different cafés, so he set out to visit each one. About halfway through the day of dropping in and out of cafés to test the coffee, one after another, he suddenly realized that something else was happening at every Italian café he visited. People were meeting, talking, joking, arguing about politics, and enjoying time together over this better-tasting cup of coffee. Schultz says it was a true epiphany when he realized there was an *emotional* Need that was being met in those cafés in Milan, but not in the U.S. It was at that moment that the Starbucks brand, as we know it today, was born.

The better-tasting cup of coffee was the *functional* Need that Starbucks filled, but that alone would never have skyrocketed Starbucks to the kind of global success the company has enjoyed. Instead, it was the *emotional* Need that Starbucks filled — the rewarding opportunity to give yourself a coffee experience, sit on a couch, relax, and enjoy your laptop or the company of others — that is responsible for its remarkable fame and fortune.

In the last chapter, we looked at the Snickers candy bar brand Target Group, but we left out the Needs that the brand fills for its customers. Knowing what we know now about Needs, let's look at how my colleagues, Richard and Mike, define the Snickers Target Group Need:

They need… one dependable snack that will always relieve their hunger and satisfy their craving for a real indulgence.

You can see here that the functional Need is "one dependable snack that's going to always relieve their hunger." And the emotional Need? That's the "craving for a real indulgence." Snickers fills both the emotional and functional Needs very well.

Just like Howard Schultz, uncovering emotional Needs can be a kind of epiphany for you, too, and filling these Needs is what will truly differentiate your brand from your competition.

Changing Needs

Imagine owning a company that makes film for cameras. If your company were to continue doing nothing but make film, eventually you'd lose almost all of your Target Group. After all, today, very few people need a camera that uses film. In these days of rapid-fire technological advances, many products and services are becoming obsolete on a regular basis, and companies that don't pay attention to these changes are becoming obsolete as well. IBM Selectric typewriters, *Encyclopaedia Britannica* hardbound books, fax machines, and audio cassette players are product examples. As for service businesses, telephone operators, gas station attendants, and walk-in travel agents are all professions that have almost been wiped out due to changing technology.

McDonald's is a good example of a company that *has* responded to the changing Needs of its Target Group by creating healthier menu items for those customers who are trying to eat less fat and fewer fried foods. McDonald's added salads to its menu and even veggie burgers in some areas for people who want to cut down on their meat consumption. McDonald's changed as the nutritional awareness of its customers changed, and in the process, it was able to meet both functional and emotional Needs of its customers.

As Bob Dylan said, "The times, they are a-changin'." In fact, change is just about the only thing you can count on for sure in today's hectic and fast-paced business world. With that in mind, you can see why staying on top of changes in the market — and in your Target Group — is fundamental to success.

Challenge yourself to know who your customers are and how their lives are changing. That will tell you how their Needs are changing, too.

The bottom line is that the best brands and business owners respond to changing Needs very quickly. It takes flexibility, but I also believe it's one of the most exciting aspects of being responsible for a brand!

The NEEDle in Your Target Group Haystack

If you take the time to work on the six components of your Target Group, focusing on your Target of One, the functional and emotional Needs of your group won't be like a needle in a haystack. They'll probably be obvious to you — hopefully, a bit more like a blinking neon sign.

Here's an example that I inferred from a company called California Wow, a fitness center. Based on reviewing their website, promotional materials, newspaper ads, facilities, etc., here's how I inferred their Target Group:

"Urban and social singles, aged 18-29, who are into everything trendy and fashionable. Their work is important to them, but their social life is truly pivotal to the quality of their lives. To stay in touch with others, they talk on the phone, SMS, e-mail, blog, and spend time on social networks on a daily basis. They love to be surrounded by music, and they spend a lot of time with friends at the movies or at clubs. They want to be in good shape physically because they know it's healthier, but even more important to them is to look great in the latest fashions."

What about current usages and behaviors? Here's what I think:

> "This Target Group doesn't exercise a great deal, but they know they should since regular exercise will keep them looking good. Right now, they get most of their exercise by walking around the city or dancing when they're at a club."

Now that I understand those aspects of California Wow's Target Group, I get a much better picture of what this group's Needs are:

> "An inexpensive, fun, hip fitness club where they can get a great workout, can see and be seen, and meet new friends in the process."

Allow the six components of a Target Group to give *you* all the clues you need to understand and define both the functional and emotional Needs of your Target Group.

7

"Frame" Your Competition

Core Positioning Element #3 — Competitive Framework

"I have been up against tough competition all my life. I wouldn't know how to get along without it."
— WALT DISNEY, CO-FOUNDER OF WALT DISNEY PRODUCTIONS

THE NEXT CORE POSITIONING ELEMENT in your Positioning Statement — Competitive Framework — is a powerful tool to help you think outside the box about who your competitors are. For that very reason, it's one of my favorite positioning elements!

Remember that your brand positioning is the way you want your customers to perceive, think, and feel about your brand *versus competition*. A lot of small businesses and solo-preneurs overlook the importance of this aspect of their positioning, trying to build their brand without spending much time or energy understanding who their competitors are and how they could be perceived differently with a Competitive Framework in mind. Big mistake! In fact, defining your Competitive Framework well makes the difference between mediocre and great brand building.

What is a Competitive Framework? Think of it as *what* your brand is. It's made up of *all* the options a customer has available to satisfy a specific need.

Here's an illustration of Competitive Framework in action. Let's say you wake up one morning with a backache. Now, if I'm a pain reliever manufacturer, I might think I have your business in the bag. As soon as you have a back ache, you're automatically going to reach for a brand like mine, right? Wrong!

There are so many other options available to you to solve your backache problem and meet your Need to ease your pain. You could stay in bed, take a hot bath, go to the doctor, get a massage, use an ice pack or heat rub, visit a chiropractor/acupuncturist, and on and on. That's an example of what Competitive Framework is all about. The more you understand the complete range of options available to respond to the Needs of your Target Group, the better you'll be able to focus your marketing and branding efforts.

Do You (Really) Know Who Your Competitors Are?

Your quick answer to this question is probably, "Yes, of course I do!" But I'd like to challenge that thinking and ask you again: How well do you *really* know them? On a scale of 1–10, for example — "1" meaning you don't know your competition at all, and "10" meaning you know your competition as well as you know your own brand — where would your response fall?

Don't feel badly if you don't score a "10." You might be surprised by how many business owners actually *don't* know their competition all that well. And, on top of that, "who" your competition is can sometimes be mighty surprising, as well!

Case in point: It isn't likely that you would consider McDonald's and Campbell's Soup to be competitors, correct? I mean, think about it: Campbell's Soup is traditionally served by opening up a can at home, pouring it into a pot on the stove, adding in water or milk, and stirring until it becomes hot. Then, you sit down at your dining room table and enjoy a nice, hot bowl of soup. So, why would McDonald's see Campbell's soup as a threat to its fast food fare?[3]

Because Campbell's introduced "Soup at Hand," an entry into the "eat-on-the-run" category. This product, sold at microwave-equipped 7-Eleven stores in ready-to-heat-and-carry packaging, became extremely popular with people on the go. Suddenly, McDonald's had to sit up and take notice of Campbell's, a competitor that Mickey D's had never had to focus on before. The competitive landscape had changed.

---

3. This information about McDonald's and Campbell's Soup comes from the article, "Do You Know Who Your Competitors Are?" by James Allen and Kara Gruver of Bain & Co., published in *Brandweek* on April 11, 2005.

Here's another example: A European candy manufacturer saw consistent drops in their sales to teens, so they conducted some research, peeling back the layers of onion to find out what was happening. What did they discover? Their biggest competitor for the teen candy segment was a cell phone company! You see, they found that the average teen had limited funds to spend, so where teens had previously spent their money on candy, they had begun spending it on texting their friends instead.

Now, you may wonder, "But aren't those two different Needs? Candy is for eating, and texting is for staying connected with friends and family. How does that fit into a Competitive Framework?" In actuality, both products filled an emotional Need for teens to "connect." The teens either had their candy after school with their friends, or they texted their friends later in the evening and on the weekends. Since these teens didn't have the money for both, candy sales suffered. Once again, you can see why staying on top of who your competitors are is fundamental to responding to the changes taking place in the market.

In yet another example, when a Thailand-based landfill company called Waste Management Siam launched its operations, its owners discovered a surprising but formidable competitor: the ground. That's right — companies in Thailand were often just burying their waste in the ground instead of turning it over to a proper waste-removal company. By getting clear on this "competitor," the company changed the entire way it operated and marketed its business. Once again, this goes to show how vital it is to understand who your competitors are — even if your competition is something other than another company!

Don't Settle For Generic

If I asked you, "What is Heineken?" you'd say, "It's a beer," right? That kind of Competitive Framework — the typical way of looking at what a brand is — is called its "Standard Identity." For example:

- Hilton is a ... *hotel.*
- Gatorade is a ... *thirst quencher.*
- McDonald's is a ... *fast food restaurant.*
- H&R Block is a ... *tax preparer.*

- Gold's Gym is a ... *fitness center.*
- Boy Scouts and Girl Scouts of America are ... *youth organizations.*
- McKinsey & Company is a ... *management consulting firm.*
- Red Cross is a ... *blood donation service.*

But — frankly speaking — aren't Standard Identities boring? If Heineken marketed itself as nothing more than a "beer," it may as well put a blank white label on the bottle. A Standard Identity is generic and not very noteworthy. It does nothing to differentiate one brand from another.

So, let's play a game to get us out of this "boring" Standard Identity mindset. It's called...

When is an Apple Not Just a Fruit?

Think of an apple's "Standard Identity." It's a fruit, right? Now, if you think of an apple as just a piece of fruit, its "competitors" would be other fruits like grapes, peaches, and bananas. Pretty straightforward.

But what if you looked at an apple in a different way? What if I said, "Actually, this apple isn't just an apple; it's an *easy-to-carry, pre-packaged kids' snack.*"

Hmm ... think about that. Is it? Sure it is! And if you looked at an apple in that way, what other types of products would that apple compete with? Cookies, crackers, potato chips, granola bars, and Snickers bars — anything that a kid could carry around in a backpack and eat quickly.

Let's take this a bit further. This time, if I were to say, "Actually, this isn't just an apple; it's a *daily health maintenance provider,*" would that be true, too? Yes! (I can hear that old phrase running through my head, "An apple a day keeps the doctor away.") If you thought of an apple in that way, it would then compete against vitamins, drinking lots of water, and getting plenty of sleep.

Let's go even further outside the realm of "Standard Identity" and say, "An apple isn't just a fruit; it's a *colorful table decoration.*" (If you'd ever seen my mother's dining room table, you'd know this is true as well.) Suddenly, that apple is competing against candles, flowers, and any number of other decorative table items.

Do you see what just happened there? That exercise is about thinking outside the box with regard to "who" your competitors truly are. By changing the way your brand is perceived and getting your customers to see your brand in a whole new light, your competition shifts, and new volume and growth opportunities readily open up.

This new way of thinking is labeled "Perceptual Competitive Framework," and I credit my good friends and colleagues, Richard Czerniawski and Mike Maloney of Brand Development Network International, with this eye-opening way of looking at your brand in a whole new light.

Brands That "Expand"

Keeping "Perceptual Competitive Framework" in mind and looking back at the brands we mentioned earlier, let's consider Hilton. Its Standard Identity is a "hotel," but it wants to be perceived as a "great getaway destination." What about the others?

- Gatorade isn't just a thirst quencher; *it's the ultimate liquid athletic equipment.*
- McDonald's isn't just a fast food restaurant; *it's a family fun and food destination.*
- H&R Block isn't just a tax preparer; *it's an affordable tax solution provider.*
- Gold's Gym isn't just a fitness center; *it's a facility for healthy and holistic strength.*
- Boy Scouts and Girl Scouts of America aren't just youth organizations; *they are developers of tomorrow's exceptional citizens.*
- McKinsey & Company isn't just a management consulting firm; *it's a premier business solutions partner.*
- Red Cross isn't just a blood donation service; *it's a humanitarian care provider in time of need.*

Let's reflect on McDonald's for a moment. If you only think of it as a fast food restaurant, its competitors are other fast food chains like Burger King, KFC, and Taco Bell. However, when you go beyond that Standard Identity and think of it as a "family fun and food destination," its competitors include zoos, parks, amusement parks, movie theaters, and more. Do you see how this expands the opportunities for sales volume for McDonald's? Of course, this change in Perceptual Competitive Framework doesn't just "happen." McD's made a concerted effort to be perceived as a family fun and food destination by adding playgrounds to their restaurants, introducing Happy Meals with free toys, and offering birthday parties for kids, just to name a few of their activities.

Does this work for a service company, too? You bet. A company called Santa Fe has grown faster than its competition by getting customers to perceive it as more than just a "moving company." If it only focused on being a moving company, it would only move things like furniture and other belongings, and it would compete only with other furniture moving companies.

But Santa Fe changed its Competitive Framework to "Relocation Services Specialist," allowing it to offer a variety of new services. Now, the company provides its clients with help to find a home, rent furniture, arrange for cross-cultural training when moving to a new country, hire domestic staff, find a handyman, arrange for an immigration visa, and even find schools for children. You can understand now why Santa Fe's business is growing!

Your Perceptual Competitive Framework

You can do the same. All it takes is a new way of thinking to help your customers perceive, think, and feel about your brand in a whole new way.

Let's say your business is a "delivery service." Boring! What if your customers saw you instead as a "valuables transporter," a "peace of mind provider," or a "last-minute savior"?

Perhaps your business is accounting, and you currently think of yourself as a "CPA." That's yawn-inducing. Instead, why not label yourself a "financial solutions partner," "a government liaison," or "an accounting department for small businesses?"

What if you own and run a small, private boutique hotel? You could be a "weekend getaway destination," a "secluded honeymoon paradise," a "business traveler's dream," or a "week-long refuge from the rat race."

Can you see how this kind of thinking expands your volume potential? I hope it's clear how establishing a Perceptual Competitive

Framework is not only hugely beneficial, but is one of the most exciting and creative activities you can undertake as a brand owner. Figuring out how you get customers to see you from a different perspective can strengthen your brand. And the beauty of it is: It doesn't have to cost you a thing.

Switching from Standard Identity to Perceptual Competitive Framework

Here's a thought process that can help you shift from only thinking in Standard Identity terms about your brand to using a Perceptual Competitive Framework.

First, ask yourself what your brand's Standard Identity is and then consider: If you only thought of your brand in those (boring) terms, who would your competitors be? Make a list.

Now that you've got that out of your system, let's make the shift to the Perceptual Competitive Framework. If you could get your Target Group to think of your brand as something else, what would that "something else" be? Once your Target Group sees you in that light, who would your competitors be?

Use your creativity, have fun with this, and remember: An apple is not just a fruit!

8

WHAT HAVE YOU DONE FOR ME LATELY?

Core Positioning Element #4 — Benefits

"Somewhere someone is looking for exactly what you have to offer."
— LOUISE HAY, AUTHOR AND PUBLISHER

WE'VE COVERED the first three core elements of your brand's positioning: Target Group, Needs, and Competitive Framework. As I explained earlier, these are the elements that come from "outside" your brand. Now, we're going to turn to the first of the "inside" elements of your brand: Benefits. This is where the rubber hits the road when it comes to branding. After all, your Target Group's primary question about your brand is: *What's in it for me?*

What are "Benefits?" They are the most meaningful promises that your brand wants to — and can — own in the mind of your Target Group.

"Promises" may seem like strange language to use when you're talking about a brand. Most of the time, we think of *people* making promises, right? But, if you think about it, brands are just like people. We build relationships with them. So, the best brands — just like the best people — keep their promises. In fact, the single most powerful way to build a strong brand is to deliver on the promises you make on behalf of your brand. As a business owner, honestly, if you don't plan to do that, you might as well save yourself time, money, and headaches, and close up shop immediately.

In This Brand We Trust

A few years back, I was shopping with a friend who had just had her second baby. She needed some cotton swabs, so we walked into a drug store where she immediately reached for the Q-Tips brand. As a brander, I was curious about her choice, which was clearly a habit for her. So, I picked up a box myself, saw that it contained 500 cotton swabs, and that it cost $2.99. I turned the box over to read what these cotton swabs were made of: cotton and sticks — nothing more.

As I put that container back on the shelf, I saw a private label, store-branded container of cotton swabs right next to the Q-Tips box. Curious, I looked at the label on the store brand, noticing that it also contained 500 cotton swabs, but cost only $1.59. What were they made of? Exactly the same as the Q-Tips: cotton and sticks. So, I turned to my friend and said, "Are you crazy? Do you realize these two products are essentially *identical*? You're going to pay almost double for the Q-Tips brand even though both boxes contain the exact same thing!"

She smiled at me, went to the checkout counter, and purchased the Q-Tips cotton swabs anyway.

This illustrates clearly that branding isn't just about a "product" that a customer buys. In the case of my friend, it was about another "ingredient" that was inside that box of Q-Tips, and that ingredient was *trust*. She trusted that Q-Tips would live up to its promises, and she didn't want to take any risks on a cheaper brand when it came to cleaning her precious baby's ear. My friend remained loyal to the brand because of that trust. You might say she had developed a *relationship* with that brand over the years, a relationship based on the brand's Benefits — its promises made and kept. So, the price difference didn't matter to her.

That's how powerful a brand promise can be when it's managed right. I suspect you'd like this for your brand as well. So, let's talk about how to get *your* brand's Benefits right.

Function and Emotion ... Again!

How do you figure out your brand's Benefits? The good news is: You've already done a lot of the heavy lifting when it comes to defining your own Benefits. That's because two chapters ago, you outlined your Target

Group's Needs, and *your brand's Benefits should be mirror images of your customers' Needs.* They are like two sides of the same coin, so the Needs section of your Target Group definition will be a key driver for your Benefits section.

Remember that Needs come in two forms: functional and emotional. Since Benefits mirror Needs, it makes perfect sense that Benefits must also be both functional and emotional.

Let's look at a recognizable brand Benefit as an example. When you think of Volvo, what's the first word that comes to mind? If you're like most people in the world, you will say "safety." That one-word Benefit is what sets Volvo apart from Mercedes Benz, Chrysler, Toyota, and all other car brands in the market. Volvo has done such a great job of establishing that single-minded brand image that it's probably perceived as the safest line of cars available around the world.

But here's a question for you: Is safety a functional Benefit or an emotional one? In many ways, it's both. Safety is a functional benefit because Volvo is built to help keep you and your family physically safe in case of an accident. But it also helps you *feel* safe and secure, knowing that you'll be okay no matter what happens. That's a strong emotional Benefit.

The best brands offer both types of Benefits. Let's look at some examples:

- Consider the Bubble Wrap brand — the plastic packaging with bubbles inside of it. Its functional Benefit is to protect fragile items during shipment. The emotional Benefit? Feeling confident that your cousin Betty's wedding present will arrive in one piece, not ten. That powerful emotional connection is what makes that brand great.

- Here's another example from an extraordinary man who lives in Thailand. Several years ago, when he saw that HIV was having a terrible impact on his beloved country, he decided to do something about it. He knew that he had to make the use of condoms educational and fun in order to break down cultural barriers and discuss what is typically considered an uncomfortable topic. So, he created a restaurant brand called Cabbages and Condoms. This restaurant serves tasty Thai food, but all of the profits go to HIV research and education charities. Eating at this restaurant is quite an experience! Everywhere you look, there is funny condom art on the walls and even woven into the rugs. In fact, at the end of your meal, instead of getting an after-dinner mint, you get — yep, you guessed it — a condom. The restaurant is now very popular among both Thais and tourists. So, what are the functional and emotional Benefits of the Cabbages and Condoms brand? Functionally, it offers tasty, traditional Thai food in a fun atmosphere. Emotionally, it allows people to feel good that they have supported a worthy cause.

- The Hard Rock Café has restaurants all across the globe and is another brand that offers very clear functional and emotional Benefits. Functionally, it offers excellent classic American food, no matter where you are in the world. Emotionally, it allows you to feel "connected" to your favorite rock stars through its signature memorabilia adorning the walls. Such memorabilia can range from Elvis Presley's pistol to Bob Dylan's guitar.

- Annie Jennings PR is a public relations business based in the U.S. that represents experts, authors, and speakers. How does it set itself apart from other PR firms? The firm's functional Benefit is excellent quality media coverage that you only have to pay for if you get booked. Their service differs from most other PR firms that charge a flat fee every single month, no matter whether you get booked or not. The emotional Benefit? You feel smart, knowing that you're getting the biggest bang for your buck and not wasting money on publicity that might never come.

The Case for Conscious Redundancy

As I said before, your Target Group Needs and the Benefits your brand offers are two sides of the same coin. They really need to match up, so aim for "conscious redundancy." Let's go back to Snickers for an example of how the Needs and Benefits elements of your brand's positioning can — and should — match up as closely as possible.

If you recall, Snickers' Needs were: "I need a dependable, solid snack that will always relieve my hunger and satisfy my craving for a real indulgence." What are the Benefits of Snickers? "Snickers is a dependable, solid snack that will always relieve your hunger and satisfy your craving for a real indulgence."

See what I mean? The two phrases are almost identical, and that's a good thing! So, don't worry if the words you use for Needs and Benefits are exactly the same. In this case, it's the right approach.

Diving Into Emotions

As I said in the chapter on Needs, a lot of brand owners feel that functional Needs are easier to uncover than emotional Needs. The same holds true for Benefits. Coming up with your brand's emotional Benefits may seem more challenging to you than deciding on your functional (tangible) Benefits.

In fact, many an SME brand owner has said to me, "But, Brenda, we're an industrial company — a manufacturer. What emotional Benefits could we possibly have or even want?"

Branding Myth:
*"B2B's and industrial companies have no emotional Benefits
to offer their customers."*

Nothing could be further from the truth! Read my lips: *Every* brand needs an emotional Benefit. That's because your customers are human beings, and human beings make choices based on feelings — even when choosing something as seemingly "tangible" as a concrete supplier, for example. Every brand must have defined emotional Needs and Benefits in order to be truly successful. If you don't, you're substantially limiting how much you can achieve as a brand, which, in turn, will keep your bottom line ... well, frankly, at the bottom!

So, think about how your customers *feel* when they use your brand or a competitor's brand. Dive deep into understanding what drives your customers emotionally. This helps you get clarity on the emotional Benefits your brand delivers, and that's fundamental to success.

What Are Your Benefits?

Take some time to sit down and brainstorm as many Benefits as possible for your brand. I recommend that you pull together a team of friends and colleagues to help you. The more brains, the better! Think about both functional and emotional Benefits, and consider the promises that your brand can — and wants to — own in the marketplace.

Once you have a potential list of Benefits, go back and review the Needs section for your Target Group that you worked on a couple of chapters ago. Choose the key Benefits that will best address the specific Needs of your Target — both functional and emotional. They should be the Benefits that you believe will not only be the most desirable for your Target Group but will also best fill those specific Target Group Needs.

Choices, Choices…

Once you've written down your brand's Benefits, you're in for what is often the most difficult part — making choices. You need to pick the top two or three Benefits that you want your brand to stand for.

Now, you may be thinking, "Wait a minute, Brenda! The more benefits my brand has, the better, right?" I'm afraid not. This is yet another branding myth busted.

Branding Myth:
"The more Benefits your brand has, the better."

The truth is that customers won't remember more than two or three benefits — maximum. Think about it: What if Volvo tried to stand for safety…and innovative design…and reliability…and unusual extras…and beauty. Your eyes would glaze over. You'd become confused about what the brand stands for, and you'd lose interest. Instead, Volvo made a tough choice to stand for a very clear benefit, and you have to do the same.

It isn't that you can't offer more Benefits. You certainly can. But if you do, chances are your Benefits won't be remembered by your customers because there will be too many of them. So, decide what one or two promises you want to stand for, and stay consistent. That's how you become the "Volvo" of *your* industry or category.

9

PROVE IT!

Core Positioning Element #5 — Reasons Why

"To be persuasive, we must be believable; to be believable, we must be credible..."

— EDWARD R. MURROW, U.S. BROADCASTER
AND JOURNALIST

PICTURE THIS IN YOUR MIND: You're in a court of law, standing before a judge who holds a gavel in his hand, and you say, "This is the promise I make with my brand." You list the brand Benefits you just defined — the unique promises your brand can, and wants to, own. The judge glares down at you, pointing his finger right in your face, and says, "Prove it!"

In a way, your Target Group is like that judge. Your customers aren't going to believe your brand will provide the Benefits you promise unless you give them some proof. Think about it: If a face cream says it can smooth out wrinkles, why would you believe it unless there was some evidence? Mere stated claims aren't enough.

So, "Reasons Why" — the fifth Core Positioning Element — are exactly that: Reasons Why your customers should believe your brand can deliver exactly what you say it can. They support your brand Benefits (that's why they come *after* the Benefits section), and they provide "sell," not just "tell."

How important are Reasons Why? Well, picture yourself in the shampoo aisle of a supermarket. As far as you can see from one end of the aisle to the next are brightly colored bottles of different brands

69

of shampoos. Let's say that on this particular day, you've decided to buy a shampoo especially for straight hair. How do you choose from all of the options? One of the bottles has a photo of a well-known, straight-haired celebrity on the front with a testimonial from her, and yet another bottle says it contains special vitamins uniquely formulated for straight hair. The celebrity's endorsement and that special ingredient are both Reasons Why, and either of these could strongly influence your shampoo-buying decision.

Next, take yourself to the toothpaste aisle. You want to buy a toothpaste that will give you the healthiest teeth overall. One of them offers baking soda as a Reason Why, while another says that eight out of ten dentists choose its brand. Which one would you choose?

What about a situation where you're trying to choose a "service brand" like a school for your children? You might check out its accreditation, research the school's success rate in the past, the credentials of the teachers and administrators, and past awards the school has won. Those are all Reasons Why you would use to help you believe that this school is the best one for your kids.

Types of Reasons Why

You may have noticed from the examples that there are different kinds of Reasons Why. In fact, there are three primary types:

- *Product- or Service-Based Reasons Why.* This might be an ingredient, a design element, or the process you use in providing your service.

- *Experience-Based Reasons Why.* This has to do with the current and past successes the brand has had in the marketplace.

- *People-Based Reasons Why.* This typically involves an endorsement from an expert or a testimonial from a satisfied customer.

Product- or Service-Based Reasons Why. First, let's look at examples of Reasons Why that are based on an attribute of a product. Dove is famous for its ingredient of "one-quarter moisturizing cream." What does this do? It supports the Benefit that it will moisturize your skin better than the competition.

Florida's Natural orange juice uses a *source* as its product-based Reason Why. Its oranges come from its own co-op, so they actually know their growers and profile them on the company's website. Of course, this Reason Why supports the brand's desired Benefit as the freshest and most natural orange juice.

What about this type of Reason Why if your business is a service company? In that case, the "product" is actually you and your team — the people delivering the service. For example, Josie Thompson is an executive leadership and performance coach in Australia. On her website, she lists a number of Reasons Why clients should believe she's a great choice for their coach. She talks about her educational degrees and her credentials as a Master Certified Coach — the highest level of certification within the International Coach Federation. She also mentions that she was named Coach of the Year for three years in a row. Other service professions have similar industry or legal certifications, such as an accountant who is a CPA or a "Ford Qualified Mechanic" that can serve as powerful Reasons Why.

What about your brand? Do you have ingredients or credentials that differentiate your brand from competition and that form the basis for strong and differentiating Reasons Why?

Experience-Based Reasons Why. The Mayo Clinic is world-renowned for its state-of-the-art medical facilities. People from across the globe go to the Mayo Clinic because it's known for having the best and most experienced doctors and researchers on the planet. For example, it has more than 20 neurosurgeons at three different locations who perform several thousand neurosurgical procedures every year. Those are meaningful Reasons Why to choose Mayo Clinic over other hospitals.

Here's an example from my own business: Over the years, I've been fortunate enough to be hired by many outstanding and well-known companies. That list of existing and past clients serves as a differentiating experience-based Reason Why to attract other potential clients who may be considering my services. We use that list on websites, in brochures, in media kits, and lots of other promotional materials.

Another type of experience-based Reason Why — leveraging associations — has been used successfully by an executive search firm called Opus Recruitment Limited. This firm, located outside the United States, formed an association with Horton International, one of the world's leading executive search groups. With Horton's more than 30 offices in the Americas, Europe, and Asia Pacific, Opus' alliance with the group helped create a great Reason Why. As a result, Opus, a much smaller recruitment firm, was able to get more business beyond their typical country borders.

What about using the longevity of a company as a Reason Why? Coors Brewery, for example, has been operating since 1873, and they tout that in their advertising and on their packaging. That kind of longevity tells you that they have maintained quality for well over a century, which, in turn, says a lot for their beer. Do keep in mind, though: Your business doesn't have to be centuries old for this type of Reason Why to have an impact on your customers. Web design companies that have been around since 1999 are considered "old!"

Awards that you, your business, or your brand have won can be additional strong experience-based Reasons Why. Case in point: Hester Creek Estate Winery in British Columbia, Canada, is one of the most award-winning wineries around, and you can bet they list all of those awards (page after page of them) on their website. If your business or prod uct has won an award, talk about it! That kind of accolade can really set you apart from your competition and give your Target Group a strong reason to believe in your Benefits.

People-Based Reasons Why typically come in two forms: testimonials or endorsements. The key is to find a true "expert" in your business area so that there is a strategic link. That person can serve as a credible voice when it comes to talking about your brand. For example, if you sell a line of makeup, you might look for an endorsement from a well-known professional makeup artist. If you're an orthopedic surgeon, testimonials from your patients who are local college hero-athletes would help your Target Group believe in the Benefits you offer. A physical therapist, hotel, or law firm may have reviews, testimonials, or articles that have been written about them, and these can easily be leveraged as Reasons Why.

Here's another example of a meaningful endorsement: A few years back, Bristol-Myers Squibb asked Lance Armstrong to endorse its cancer drugs — the very same drugs that kept him alive and allowed him to get back into shape as a competitive rider. Without those drugs, Lance wouldn't have become a seven-time winner of the Tour de France. It's that kind of meaningful connection that made all the difference in "proving" the effectiveness of Bristol-Myers Squibb's cancer drugs.

Guess What? You Already Have Reasons Why

Now, you may be saying, "But, Brenda, I'm a small local business. I don't know anyone famous to promote my brand!" No problem — you don't have to.

In fact, for every happy customer you have, you already have a great Reason Why. Leveraging client testimonials from your existing or past customers is an immediate and effective way to convince potential clients that you can deliver your promised Benefits.

Let's say you're a local dentist, and you take pride in creating an environment which eases the usual nerves people feel when they have dental work done. Leverage that as a point of differentiation by interviewing past clients about their experiences. Get them to share how they felt more comfortable and less nervous in your office. Then, transcribe their words and use them on your website, in brochures, and any other marketing materials you produce to support your practice. That's how you become *the* choice for potential patients who want to have a nerve-free dental experience.

The key to successfully getting testimonials is to ask for one as soon as possible after your customers have used your product or service. This way, the experience will be fresh in their minds. And be sure to make it easy for your customers to give you a testimonial, too. For instance, maybe a customer would prefer to simply "speak" their testimonial to you rather than write it down. If that's the case, record it on an audio device, and transcribe it later.

I once had a client who was happy to give me a testimonial but was strapped for time to write it. So, we agreed that I would interview him by phone, type up his key points, and send the draft testimonial to him for approval. Once he approved it, his secretary put it on his letterhead, and voilà! I had a testimonial in a fraction of the time it would've taken if I had waited for him to find the time to do it himself.

How about having a location on your website where people can automatically write a testimonial for you? Better yet, whenever you can, get *video* testimonials, and post them on your YouTube Channel and website. If your business is brick and mortar, leave comment cards at checkout counters for customers to complete.

Here are a couple of additional tips about testimonials:

- When requesting the testimonial, ask your customers to be as specific as possible about why they found your service or product to be superior. Ask them to articulate what really made your brand stand out.

- Get the person's name and title, and ask for their permission to print it. That adds even stronger credibility.

The bottom line is: Testimonials are important Reasons Why, and fortunately, you have as many potentially good testimonials as you have satisfied customers! This type of Reason Why is right at your fingertips — and for almost no cost. All you have to do is ask.

The Reasons Why Trifecta

If you can, use all three types of Reasons Why to support your brand benefits, and you'll be surprised how fast your brand will grow.

The Yonex brand of tennis racket is a case in point. My personal trainer's brother, Dave, aspires to be a professional tennis player and is in the market to buy a new tennis racquet. He's considering the Yonex brand because he's been told it "delivers more power to meet the needs of the sports world." That sounds great, but why should he believe that promise?

- The *product-based* Reason Why for Yonex is that it's the only ultra-light isometric tennis racquet created with a nickel titanium alloy in its shaft. This allows a full transfer of power from the racquet to the ball.

- The *experience-based* Reason Why for Yonex is that it's the first and only brand of tennis racquet to be used to win both the French Open and Wimbledon.

- Yonex's *people-based* Reasons Why come in the form of endorsements by famous professional tennis players like Monica Seles, Lleyton Hewitt, and Martina Hingis.

Can you see how using all three types of Reasons Why combined together can make your brand hard to beat?

Keep Those Reasons Why Linked to Benefits

I mentioned this earlier, but it merits repeating. Your Reasons Why *must* be linked to your Benefits. That's their whole reason for being. In fact, a Benefit without a Reason Why is like an airplane without wings — it just isn't going to take off.

What about a spa that says it offers the following Benefits: "Expert healing massages in a pampering environment to help you reduce stress." Let's take a look at each benefit and see what Reasons Why the spa offers for each:

- The benefit of expert healing massages is supported because they have registered massage therapists on staff with an average of five years' experience. The spa is also recommended by the city's Association of Physical Therapists.

- The benefit of a pampering environment is supported in that all clients are provided with a plush robe and ergonomic spa slippers.

- The benefit of helping to reduce stress is supported because all of the rooms at the spa have aromatherapy, gentle lighting, and piped-in, nature-based music.

Can you see how the Benefits and Reasons Why match up?

Benefits		Supporting Reasons Why
Expert Healing Massages	→	Registered therapists with five or more years of experience
		Recommended by the Association of Physical Therapists
Pampering Environment	→	Plush robe
		Ergonomic spa slippers
Stress Reduction	→	Aromatherapy
		Gentle lighting
		Relaxing music

Your Brand's Reasons Why

Revisit the Benefits you selected for your brand in the last chapter, and ask yourself why your customers should believe that your brand can deliver those Benefits. Brainstorm Reasons Why of all types until you have a long list of potential ones. This is one of those situations where you definitely want to ask others for help because, when it comes to brainstorming Reasons Why, the more brains, the better. If you're a very small company or a solo-preneur without many or any staff members, ask friends, family, and former colleagues to help. Take them out for lunch or a drink, and get the creative juices flowing.

Here are some questions to ask to help you come up with good Reasons Why:

- Why do your current customers buy your product(s) or service(s)? (Don't know? Ask them!)

- What is unique and different about the way your product is designed? Are there special ingredients in your product that deliver the Benefits you want to own?

- What is particularly efficient or effective about the way your service process works? How is your service differentiated from the competition?

- What endorsements could you get from a third party that would be not only strategic but also very meaningful to your Target Group?

- What awards, credentials, affiliations, education, or experience do you have that could provide impressive Reasons Why?

Once you've created a long list of Reasons Why, it's time to choose the most meaningful ones. Here again, you have to make tough decisions, so how do you go about it? One important hint: Be sure you don't choose the Reasons Why that *you* think are most meaningful! Remember to choose the ones that will be the most meaningful to *your Target Group*. In this instance, as a brand owner, it actually doesn't matter much what *you* think.

By the way, don't assume you know what matters to your customers. Instead, find out from them directly. Put together a survey online or on paper. List the Benefits your brand wants to own with all of the possible

Reasons Why, and ask your customers to vote on which Reasons Why are the most compelling to support their belief in those Benefits. You could also host a mini-focus group at a dinner or take some customers to lunch to get their opinions. If you're close enough to your best customers, call them on the phone, and ask for a few moments of their time to chat about it.

Don't Let Your Reasons Why Grow Stale

Make sure to revisit your Reasons Why every six months or so. You may have new Reasons Why evolving that could further build your brand. Did you add a new ingredient, win a recent award, or obtain a great new testimonial? Don't let a valuable Reason Why slip through your fingers!

10

DOES YOUR BRAND HAVE PERSONALITY?

Core Positioning Element #6 — Brand Character

"You now have to decide what 'image' you want for your brand. Image means personality. Products, like people, have personalities, and they can make or break them in the market place."
— DAVID OGILVY, ADVERTISING ICON

YOU HAVE NOW REACHED the sixth and last Core Positioning Element of your Positioning Statement — "Brand Character." Think of Brand Character as the *personality* of your brand — its demeanor, disposition, and overriding attitude. Brand Character is important and can help differentiate brands that are otherwise seen as similar. It gives customers yet another reason to choose one brand over another and also helps build a relationship between a brand and its customer.

Take Coke and Pepsi. As I mentioned before, these two brands are pretty much identical from a product standpoint. Inside each can, you will find carbonated water, a little bit of flavoring, and sweetener. But if I ask someone which cola they prefer, 9 times out of 10, that person will have a very strong point of view. Why? I believe it comes down to Brand Character.

Brands With Character

Let's use your imagination to bring the Coke and Pepsi Brand Characters to life. Pretend you're in a room with two doors. Standing in one of those doorways is Coke — the brand — but as a *person*. In the other doorway stands Pepsi — the brand — also as a person. What would those two people look like? How are they different? Which one is younger? Which one is older? How do these two different people dress? What are their attitudes? Those differences you have highlighted in your mind are driven by Brand Character, and that's how you differentiate brands that are similar to one another from a product or service standpoint.

Let's compare some other brands that are similar in product but very different in Brand Character. Remember: Just as every person on the face of the planet has different DNA, no two brands are ever the same either.

Consider ads from two different fragrances: Fendi and Coco Mademoiselle. A Fendi ad contains three photographs of a model who looks to be in various stages of ecstasy. This ad is sexy, but it's a sensual, passionate kind of sexy. A Coco Mademoiselle perfume ad, on the other hand, shows a model lounging in a beautiful dress with a bottle of the perfume in the foreground. You would probably consider this ad sexy, as well, but it's a more sophisticated, less obvious kind of sexy.

The point is that you have to be specific when you describe Brand Character. Describing these two perfumes as just "sexy" isn't enough.

The same is true of advertisements for Grey Goose and Smirnoff vodka brands. One of Grey Goose's ads contains just an image of the bottle and two glasses against a topaz blue background. This communicates a Brand Character that is elegant, sophisticated, classic, and clean. Smirnoff, on the other hand, has an ad with a group of people in business suits sitting on a ledge. Through the bottle of Smirnoff, however, we see an overweight man in his underwear also sitting on the ledge. That's hardly an "elegant" Brand Character! Instead, it's surprising, playful, and humorous. Both of these brands are just vodka — roughly the same liquid in a bottle — but their very different Brand Characters help to drive their positionings in the marketplace and will appeal to different Target Groups.

Now, let's look at the Brand Character of a *service* business. I once visited the office of a public relations agency located overseas, and the Managing Director shared with me his firm's Brand Character: "Thoughtful, approachable, and friendly, but honest and realistic. Calm and rational in approach, helpful and creative. Quiet confidence with a hidden edge."

As we were chatting in the agency's conference room, the Managing Director pointed to a variety of unique and "quirky" visuals hanging on the wall. He explained to me that he had told each member of his team that they could hang anything they wanted there as long as it represented that specific individual and his or her own unique creativity. Customers come in, look at the pictures, and immediately realize that the PR firm's staff is clearly very creative. It's a great way of communicating the agency's Brand Character, and it is indeed the "hidden edge" that the Managing Director told me about. As I left that office, I turned around and looked again. The entrance felt honest, realistic, calm, and rational. I admire how they have embraced their Brand Character even through their office choice and design.

Insurance companies — another type of service business — also use Brand Character as a way of differentiating themselves from one another. After all, insurance products are reasonably similar, too, right? So, each company has to find a way to stand out from the others. If you've seen advertisements for the AFLAC brand of insurance, you'll know that this company runs commercials with an outspoken duck that creates a fun and engaging Brand Character but also drives home the point that the company cares about you as an individual.

Compare AFLAC with Liberty Mutual, another insurance company with a very different Brand Character. In one of their commercials, they show a series of scenarios in which people voluntarily help each other and even save each other from near injury. This presents a Brand Character for Liberty Mutual of "helpful" and "responsible."

"Who" is Your Brand?

Hopefully, you can see how impactful Brand Character can be as a differentiator to help you find your own unique position in the marketplace. So, how do you go about it? Keep in mind that defining a Brand Character isn't necessarily about your *current* Brand Character; it's about the Brand Character you *desire* for your brand. If you don't yet have the Brand Character you want, you have something to work toward.

The key to talking about Brand Character is to describe your brand using the same types of personality characteristics that you would use to describe people. If your brand were a person standing in a doorway, how would you describe it?

Try flipping through magazines for pictures of people you feel represent your brand's personality and attitude. (While you're at it, also look for pictures that you believe do *not* represent your brand's personality and attitude. It's just as important to know what you don't want to stand for as it is to know what you *do* want to stand for!)

Once you've gathered a few photos, look at each one, and ask yourself what specific words best describe the personality you carved out in those images. Are these words appropriate for your Brand Character?

- Use **descriptive words and phrases** like street-smart, outgoing, wise, practical, professional, rebellious, or no-nonsense. I suggest avoiding words like "authoritative" or "reliable." These words are, frankly, a bit ordinary and expected. The more unique and distinctive your description, the more ownable your Brand Character will be, and the more likely you'll capture the attention of your Target Group as compared to your competition.

- You can also write a **personal narrative** that describes your Brand Character. For example, the Brand Character for a company of virtual assistants I know came up with this for their Brand Character: "Perfectionists you can always depend on to do the job right the first time."

Here is a list of adjectives that you can use as a starting point. Cross out the words that don't apply, and keep the words that do. Feel free to add more words as they come to you.

Irreverent	Serene	Dedicated
Chic	Earnest	Even-tempered
Street-wise	Sparkling	Decisive
Authentic	Soulful	Vivacious
Maverick	Eloquent	Generous
Professional	Soft-spoken	Rascal
Focused	Gregarious	Spiritual
Gracious	Grounded	Considerate
Altruistic	Industrious	Sociable
Fair-minded	Courageous	Visionary
Colorful	Approachable	Daring

Magnetic	Whimsical	Ethical
Inspirational	Direct	Compassionate
Engaging	Wise	Encouraging
Influential	Persuasive	Passionate
Reliable	Trustworthy	Steadfast

Remember that you are defining your Brand Character the way you want to create it in the minds of your customers. So, go back to the Target Group portion of your Positioning Statement, and ask yourself: Would my Target Group find these words or this description appealing? That's of vital importance, and that's how you make sure your brand isn't "bland."

11

PULLING IT ALL TOGETHER
Your Brand's Complete Positioning Statement

"Details create the big picture."
— SANFORD I. WEILL, BANKER, FINANCIER,
AND PHILANTHROPIST

CONGRATULATIONS! YOU HAVE DEFINED the six elements of your brand positioning. The next step is not only the #1 way to leverage your brand positioning, but it's also the least expensive, simplest, and most effective:

Write it down.

Now, I realize you may be thinking, "Do I really need to write it down?" Dozens of people have said to me over the years: "Brenda, I have defined my six elements now, so I'm ready to go!" That's great, but since they never took the time to incorporate all six elements into a cohesive, written whole, that positioning never became central to their business. Even worse, it was never fine-tuned enough to *build* their business.

Writing down your positioning makes it *actionable* so that you can share it with your team. Then, and only then, will it become a strategic document that allows everyone to help drive your brand's growth.

Turning the six elements of a positioning into a strategic document — a Brand Positioning Statement — is what this chapter is all about. Now that you have defined all six elements of your positioning, committing them to an "official" Brand Positioning Statement is another powerful, yet low-cost, way to serve your brand day in and day out.

This is the same process that has worked for the world's most successful billion-dollar brands, and it will work for your brand as well. Having a solid and crystal-clear Brand Positioning Statement is truly the secret ingredient behind successful branding.

Positioning Statement Example #1: California Wow

Let's take a look at a couple of service businesses to see how the pieces fit together to form very different Positioning Statements, even though these businesses are in the same industry. Both of these businesses are fitness centers, and I inferred their positionings from information I've researched about them.

California Wow Fitness Center Inferred Positioning Statement

Target Group:

Demographics, Psychographics, Attitudes

Urban, social, single, aged 18-29, trendy, fashionable, and "in the know" about all that's going on. Their work is important to them, but their social life is pivotal to the quality of their lives. To stay in touch with others, they talk on the phone, SMS, e-mail, and blog regularly. They love to be surrounded by music and use iPods while walking on the street, taking the commuter train, etc. They eat out with friends on the weekends, go to movies, and go clubbing where they enjoy dancing, meeting others, and checking out fashions. They want to be in healthy shape physically because they know it's good for them, and they want to look great in what they wear. So, they try to exercise whenever they can, but they want to enjoy their exercise time. This means that exercise needs to be inexpensive, and their friends and other social people need to be around to make it fun for them.

Current Usage and Behaviors

They don't exercise much right now, but they know they should, not only for health but because regular exercise will keep them looking good. Right now, they get most of their exercise through walking and through dancing when clubbing with friends.

Needs (Functional and Emotional):

An inexpensive, "hip," and fun fitness club where they can get a great workout, can see and be seen, and meet new friends in the process.

Is the Brand of (Competitive Framework):

Hip and fun workout experience. Competing primarily with: Dancing, clubbing, other fitness facilities.

That Provides (Benefits):

The city's funnest, hippest, and most social exercise facility at a good value.

Because (Reasons Why):

- State-of-the-art fitness equipment in 48,000 square feet of space

- 8 different club locations with interchangeable membership

- Fun Start/Fit Start Program

- Membership available for as low as $20 per month

- Energetic, beautiful personal trainers who are not only well-trained but who make working out fun

- The fitness center where the most celebrities and models belong

- Other fun group exercise alternatives such as Punch! Kick! Jump! classes

- Energetic music piped throughout the club all day and night

The Brand Character is:

Trendy, fun, outgoing, and social. The kind of person you love to go clubbing with. In great shape, popular, and good looking. Aspirational.

• • • •

Can you see how this Positioning Statement gives you a clear picture of what the California Wow brand stands for, who they want to attract to the club, and how the club differentiates itself in the marketplace?

Positioning Statement Example #2: Cascade Club

Cascade Club Fitness Center Inferred Positioning Statement

Target Group:
Demographics, Psychographics, Attitudes
Downtown-based successful working professionals, aged 35-55, whose career pressures, long work days, and busy travel schedules leave them little free time for exercise. They strive to be the best and to surround themselves with the best in all they do. Their career successes have led them to become increasingly accustomed to the finer things in life. They understand and appreciate the importance of remaining healthy, and they know that regular exercise and maintaining a healthy lifestyle is critical to their continued success in life.

Current Usage and Behaviors
They may have access to fitness equipment either in their homes or in the workplace, and they try to work as much exercise into their schedules as they can. But it's extremely difficult to find the time, and at the end of a long work day, they often find themselves too tired to exercise. If they exercise at work or at home, they are often "torn" — reminded of responsibilities when they see colleagues and/ or their families. If they commit to, and spend good money on, joining a fitness club, they will use it.

Needs (Functional and Emotional):
They seek a top-of-the-line exercise and health club where they can get away from the pressures of their work and personal lives and focus on themselves for a while. They want the very best machines, personal trainers, and workout facilities in the city in a luxurious "pampering" environment.

Is the Brand of (Competitive Framework):
Private health and lifestyle oasis. Competing mainly with: 5-star hotel fitness clubs and spas, Fitness First, other private clubs, independent top-end spas.

That Provides (Benefits):
The city's best overall health, exercise, and lifestyle facility where you can achieve your health goals and pamper yourself in private club luxury.

Because (Reasons Why):

- State-of-the-art exercise equipment in 3,500 square meters of pristine training and fitness rooms

- Best certified personal trainers in the country for individualized goal attainment

- Full range of health, beauty, and lifestyle amenities (luxurious changing rooms, separate male and female saunas, steam and Jacuzzi rooms, accompanying spa, private poolside cabanas, wine and juice bar, and poolside dining options)

The Brand Character is:

Prestigious, exclusive, premium, luxurious. A perfectionist who desires the very best. Service-minded and supportive — a life coach who understands your needs and who will help you achieve your fitness and personal goals.

• • • •

Dare to Be Different

You can see that, even though they are in the same industry, the California Wow and Cascade Club brands are very different. They have each carved out a very specific niche or place in the market that they want to own. Each Target Group is very distinct, the needs of each Target Group are different, and these differences drive very unique positionings.

That's what you're aiming for as well. You can — and should — differentiate your brand just as clearly.

Your Current Positioning vs. Your Desired Positioning

As you work on your Brand Positioning Statement, remember that you already have a positioning in the minds of your customers. You may discover, however, that your current positioning is not what you'd like it to be. You may want to alter the perceptions, thoughts, and feelings of your Target Group in order to strengthen your brand. Remember: Your goal is to get your customers to feel that your brand is the *only* choice in the marketplace. If your current positioning doesn't accomplish this right now, then you should develop a *desired* brand positioning that you can work toward.

Completing your Brand Positioning Statement is the first step in achieving your desired positioning. It will give you a clear picture of where your brand stands right now, and it will help you determine what you need to alter — in each of the six elements — to reach your desired brand positioning goal.

Don't forget that your brand positioning is in large part about how you want to influence the mind of the consumer. You need to establish a relationship with your Target Group and give your brand personality. You want your customers to say, "I only use [your brand]," or "I would never dream of trying anything but [your brand]."

Polish Your Position

Now, it's time to take the six elements you've already worked on, and pull them all together into a format to create your own unique and distinctive positioning. Take your time, and make sure that all the pieces really fit together well. Double-check that there is a natural flow to your statement. If you have a trusted friend or advisor who could look at your Positioning Statement, get their perspective.

It's absolutely crucial to write down your Brand Positioning Statement before you move on to the next chapter, because this Statement will serve as the foundation for everything that follows. As you continue through this book, you may get more ideas to add to your positioning, and that's fine. Just be sure you have a reasonably cohesive draft before you continue.

Remember, too: By having a Brand Positioning Statement clearly defined and well written out, I guarantee you will be heads and tails above 80–90% of all SMEs and solo-preneurs out there!

Make Your Positioning Work for You

Once you have your completed Brand Positioning Statement written down, here is an important and effective, low-cost way to leverage it:

Keep it top of mind.

You should be thinking about your brand and what it stands for on a daily basis. To help you keep your positioning at the forefront of your mind, post your Positioning Statement in key locations where you have a chance to run into it regularly. Make it your screensaver, post it on your wall, keep it in your desk drawer — wherever you're most likely to run into it. It's a fundamental part of maintaining that ever-so-important "marketing mindset" we talked about.

So, your Brand Positioning Statement is front and center — what now?

Use it daily.

Your Brand Positioning Statement, used on a daily basis, will become the backbone of your brand and will help you immensely when it comes time to making decisions, day in and day out.

Let's consider this example: Say that you're the owner of a restaurant with a desired positioning of being the city's #1 high-quality, high-end business lunch locale for executives. You seek a desired brand character of "elegant, prestigious, higher priced, but worth it." One day, an employee comes to you and says, "There's going to be a neighborhood street fair in our area that will bring families in from all over the city. I think we should set up a stall and serve food." Knowing your positioning, you would quickly see that this idea doesn't fit with your desired Target Group, nor is it consistent with your Brand Character.

On the other hand, if another staff member came to you sharing the news of a large convention of business executives that will take place in your city six months from now, you might be interested in setting up a booth there and/or even arranging to provide samples of food since the convention will attract clientele within your Target Group. You would, of course, want to set up your booth in an "elegant" way to make sure the ambience of your restaurant comes through.

I've seen far too many brands fall prey to the "latest, greatest idea" syndrome, where someone you know has passion for a wild and quirky new idea, and you find yourself suddenly doing something that has nothing whatsoever to do with your desired brand. Not only is this a waste of time and money and energy, but it also could end up *hurting* your brand in the long run. It's absolutely crucial to make what you "do" with your brand consistent with what you "say" you want your brand to be.

I hope you can see now how your Brand Positioning Statement truly serves as a GPS that puts your business into motion and makes sure you stay headed in the right direction. With this document in hand, you will be able to put the next "right" idea into action to grow your business and your brand to a degree you may never have previously thought possible.

12

Don't Just Say ... Do!

Low-Cost Ways to Leverage Your Positioning Statement

"Well done is better than well said."
    –Benjamin Franklin, A Founding Father
    of the United States

You now have your Brand Positioning Statement ready, posted, and front of mind. You are crystal clear on what you "say" your brand is all about. How do you make sure you communicate that positioning effectively to your customers?

Let's look at how a couple of megabrands communicate what they want to stand for in the market.

- Stop for a minute and think about why you like your Apple iPod. If you're like me, you like it because it's easy to carry, easy to use, has good sound quality, and can contain thousands of pieces of music and videos. All of these positive things communicate to me what iPod wants to stand for: easy mobile entertainment.

- What about Volvo? I actually own a Volvo because the brand makes me feel safe. I know that Volvo engineers have built the cars to assure roof reinforcements in case of rollover collisions, and if our car gets too close to a neighboring car, a little "detector" button goes off to warn me. All of these activities and more are built into my Volvo and communicate to me what Volvo clearly stands for: safety.

What do these two examples demonstrate to you? Hopefully, you can see through these cases that…

A brand communicates what it wants to stand for not by what is "says" it is, but by what it *does*.

Let's face it: I'm never going to see either one of these brands' Positioning Statements, but I don't have to. What they are *doing* to communicate their brands helps me understand immediately what they want to stand for.

It's the same with your brand. You must consistently communicate what you want your brand to stand for by what you do, not by what you say.

Assume you have a tax management service company, and you want your brand to stand for reliability. You can "tell" your clients that you're reliable ten ways to Sunday, but those are merely words. One day, a client calls you and says, "Please get me a tax projection by 8:00 a.m. on Wednesday morning." Always eager to please, you respond, "No problem. I'm reliable!"

In this very simple case, there are a host of ways that your actions could deliver for — or against — your desired "reliable" brand:

- Instead of turning in the projection at 8:00 a.m. on Wednesday morning, you turn the projection in at 8:00 a.m. on *Tuesday* morning, a full 24 hours in advance of when it is due. That's a very different "reliable" brand than…

- …if you turn in the tax projection at 7:59 a.m. on Wednesday morning, just one minute in advance of the deadline. While you may still be on time, it transmits a different "reliable" brand than…

- …if you turn in the tax projection at 5:00 p.m. on Wednesday, with no explanation as to why it's late. In that case, you haven't communicated a "reliable" brand at all.

The bottom line? You can have a well-thought-out Brand Positioning Statement that is crystal clear and spot-on, but it will mean nothing unless you communicate it consistently in what you do, day in and day out. That's the holy grail when it comes to successful brand building.

Don't Sink Your Brand!

It's estimated that only 20% of an iceberg actually shows above the water while the remaining 80% is hidden beneath the water's surface. Your brand positioning is much the same. The 80% that your customers will never see is your Brand Positioning Statement, while the remaining 20% — the part that is out in the open for all to see — is what you *do* to communicate your positioning to your clients. Every single interaction that a customer has with your brand takes place at the upper 20% and will form the basis for how a customer perceives, thinks, and feels about your brand.

Sit back and look objectively at everything you "do" today to communicate your brand. Review your website and any public relations work you have done. Look at your brochures, merchandising, packaging, storefront (if you have one), the nature of the people you hire, your offices — everything. If you're a solo-preneur working from your home, the bulk of your communications may take place on the phone, in meetings, or via proposals. Either way, these represent the 20% of the iceberg that's above the water. Is that 20% communicating your brand the way you want?

Is Your Brand a Mutant?

If you remember one thing about effectively communicating what your brand stands for, I hope it's this: If what you "do" and what you "say" are two different things, you simply will not create a brand.

Let me explain with a medical analogy. You know from science class that the DNA of your fingernail is the same as the DNA of your skin is the same as the DNA of your hair, right? If they weren't all the same, you'd be ... a mutant!

It's the same with your brand. When people ask me, "Brenda, what does it take to build a truly blockbuster brand?" I always say two things:

1. Be crystal clear about what you want your brand to stand for.

2. Communicate that desired brand consistently, consistently, consistently every single day in everything you do.

Think about it: What would have happened if Nike had put out print ads with its famous slogan of "Just Do It" at the same time that it released television commercials showing someone wearing Nike sneakers sitting in front of the television watching sports? It's just not the same message.

Everything you do must be consistent with what you say you stand for. Think about your business cards, the tweets you send through Twitter, the posts on your Facebook page, your brochures, your website, your packaging, your e-newsletters, your blogs, your e-mails, what you say about your service in phone calls or meetings, and even the way you and/or your team members dress when meeting with clients. If any of these pieces is inconsistent, you run the risk of your customer becoming confused. If you communicate one message one day and something else the next, you might as well be speaking a foreign language to your clients. They just aren't going to understand.

Once again, that's why it's so important to create your brand's Positioning Statement. You will then have a clear picture of how you want your Target Group to perceive, think, and feel about your brand and how you can clearly communicate your positioning through every single client interaction — no matter the shape or form of that communication.

Don't Be "Anti-Social"

Speaking of various means of communication, like many business owners, you may be wondering what role social media should play in building your brand. "What specific Facebook strategy would drive the best customer loyalty? Who should manage our brand's Twitter account? How do we leverage YouTube to create the next viral video?" These are all excellent questions, especially since millions of people communicate through social media every day, and there are no signs of that stopping anytime soon. In fact:

- The number of people on Facebook is now larger than the population of the United States; at the time of this writing, if Facebook were a country, it would be the third largest in the world.

- According to OnlineMarketing-Trends.com, Twitter now has 106 million accounts and adds 300,000 users daily. These users send 55 million tweets every day.

- 25% of all web searches go to YouTube, making it the second largest search engine in the world.

Rupert Murdoch, one of the most famous publishing magnates of this century, has said that social media is the biggest shift in communications since the invention of the printing press more than 500 years ago. Despite having some of his own brand challenges in recent years, Murdoch's comment clearly underscores the important role social media plays in the way we communicate today.

So, face the facts: Social media is big, and it's here to stay! It's not only changing the way we communicate with our customers, but how they communicate with each other. So, you can't afford to be "anti-social" with your brand.

But in the midst of all this flurry of social media excitement, it's important for business leaders to sit back, take a deep breath, and remember: "How" we communicate with clients may be changing dramatically, but "what" we communicate should not change.

In truth, the means we use to communicate with our customers has changed many times over the years. In the early days of radio, business owners were excited about the potential for audio advertising. Then, television came along. Can you imagine how revolutionary that was? The types of printers have changed drastically, too, from mimeographed copies to the sophisticated home printers we use today. Throughout all of these changes, however, the keys to success have always been to know your Target Group intimately, take care of their functional and emotional Needs, and make sure your brand responds to those Needs better than the competition.

No matter how you communicate with your customers, everything you do is about gaining loyal brand users and never giving them a reason to switch to another brand. It really is that simple, whether you're creating a television ad or writing a tweet.

The buzz word I hear more and more these days when it comes to social media is "relationship." "We must build a *relationship* with our consumers using social media!" cry the marketers. But building a relationship between your brand and your customers has *always* been at the core of good brand building — day in and day out. That hasn't changed. All that is evolving is *how* you choose to build that relationship.

The great thing about social media is that it has made building relationships with your customers easier, more immediate, and less expensive. You don't need a million dollars to post on your Facebook fan page regularly! With so many social media opportunities today to interact with your customers on a regular basis, there has never been a more exciting time to build a brand. All of these tools are at your disposal at incredibly low cost. Just don't let the excitement of these new tools steer you away from the true essence of brand building. If you remember to stick to the basics, you can't go wrong.

Actions Speak Louder Than Words — A "Lofty" Example

If you live outside of Asia, you may never have heard of the Nok Air brand, but this low-cost airline is an example of a brand that has done a great job of communicating its Brand Positioning Statement through what it does. Based out of Thailand and flying across Asia, I would summarize its desired positioning in this one simple sentence:

Nok Air wants to be the most enjoyable, reliable, and affordable flying experience in Asia.

The company's management looked at every aspect of their operating structure and figured out how their brand could reflect and communicate that positioning in everything they do. Keeping in mind that "nok" means "bird" in Thai, let's review Nok Air's strategies.

Product/Service:

- Since an enjoyable flying experience starts from the moment a customer arrives at the airport, Nok Air staff members meet travelers as they enter the check-in area. Armed with a PDA, the staff can check customers in right away, shortening the time passengers spend in line.

- To continue Nok Air's enjoyable flying experience, flight attendants create fun activities on board, including doing a little "bird" dance as they go up and down the aisle, which makes passengers laugh and relax.

Employees:

- As an airline, if you want customers to have an enjoyable flying experience, you'd better choose employees who love being in the business of serving customers. With this in mind, Nok Air developed its own "Flight Attendant Reality TV Show." Attractive women from all over Thailand clamored to get on television and compete to see who would be chosen as Nok Air flight attendants. And get this: Because it was good entertainment—and millions of people watched—the television channel actually *paid* for the programming. (Talk about a low-cost or no-cost marketing and branding idea!)

- Attractive, bright yellow uniforms worn by the airline's employees also help customers enjoy their flying experience. In keeping with the fun "bird" theme, some of the brightly colored uniforms actually have wings hooked on the back!

Booking and Paying for Flights:

- Want an affordable airline ticket? Then, don't go through a travel agent. In fact, Nok Air has arranged it so that customers can buy their airline ticket at convenience stores (more convenience = more enjoyable).

- Customers can pay for their Nok Air plane tickets by mobile phone…and in installments. For a more enjoyable flight, you can go online and make your seat selection—something that a lot of other low-cost airlines don't offer.

Planes:

- How else does Nok Air brand itself as an enjoyable flying experience for passengers? The airline actually paints all of its planes so that they look like birds. The pilots sit in the "beak." I've seen young children standing in the Thai airport looking out the window at the planes on the tarmac, pleading to their parents, "Please let's fly on the 'bird airplane!'" The next time that family wants to go on a low-cost family vacation, I suspect Nok Air will be their airline of choice.

Operations:

- To hold true to its brand of "reliable flying experience," Nok Air has an on-time guarantee of 95% that it highlights in its advertising and marketing efforts.

- Nok Air has contracted with Thai Airways — the country's largest and most important airline — to manage Nok Air's airplane maintenance, further strengthening the airline's "reliable" positioning.

Do you see how all of these activities — what Nok Air *does* — fit together into one cohesive whole to communicate what the company wants to stand for?

Your Brand in a Nutshell

Creating a brief summary just like I did for Nok Air is a powerful way to make sure what you do with your brand is consistent with what you want it to be. If you could sum up your entire brand positioning in one simple sentence, what would you say?

- For example, let's go back to the Cascade Club's positioning statement. For this company, we might summarize their desired brand as something like: *The city's most luxurious private exercise and lifestyle facility.*

- W Hotel Chain's positioning summary might be: *The coolest hotels with the hippest bars in the most exciting cities around the globe.*

- H&R Block's positioning summary might be: *A fast, reliable, and affordable way to tax-filing peace of mind.*

Get the idea? How would you write your own brand's positioning summary? Take a moment to create the perfect "nutshell" statement that succinctly and strategically summarizes your brand.

Well done! You've made it through the first asset you already have — your brand positioning. Whether developing your brand positioning was an easy process or not, I hope you can see how fundamentally important it is as a key step to building a successful brand.

13

How Do Your Customers Need You? Let Us Count the Ways

Brand-Building Asset #2 — Customers: Uncovering Needs

"This may seem simple, but you need to give customers what they want, not what you think they want. And if you do this, people will keep coming back."
— John Ilhan, successful Australian entrepreneur

I'M ALWAYS SURPRISED at how many small business owners introduce new products and services to the market like they're throwing darts. They say they don't have the funds to research what the customer needs, so they just "put it out there" and wait to find out what works and what doesn't.

What happens if you do this? The products and services that don't sell well undermine the perception of your brand as a whole. And, of course, you've just wasted time and a lot of money. So, this approach is costly in many ways.

What these SMEs and solo-preneurs don't realize is that they're spending much more money on creating products and services that *won't* sell than they would spend if they just put some effort into a little low-cost, focused market research. It also takes a lot more time for your team to put a new product or service out into the marketplace than to first determine if the product has a chance of succeeding. Don't let this happen to your brand!

This is why the #2 brand-building asset you already have is: your customers. Yes, your customers are a fundamentally important asset that you can use to market your brand efficiently and effectively.

Eight Ways to Uncover Your Customers' Needs

Customers can help you build a powerful brand in a variety of ways, but the first way we'll explore is through uncovering and understanding their new, unmet, and changing Needs.

Let's face it: If your customers don't need you, there isn't much hope for your brand. Remember that marketing involves "all of the activities related to finding out what your customers **want and need** and then satisfying those Needs better than competition." So, how many ways can you count that your customers need you? If that's not perfectly clear in your mind, your ability to market your brand will be limited.

I know we already talked about Needs in your Brand Positioning Statement, but we're now going to delve deeper into how you can uncover your customers' Needs without spending lots of money. Here are just eight out of dozens of inexpensive ways you can lift the veil on what your customers need from you.

#1: Just Listen!

It may sound overly fundamental, but the #1 most inexpensive means of getting to know your customers' Needs better is simply to listen. It's so simple, in fact, that many solo-preneurs and business owners overlook it.

Let me give you an example of someone who used the simple act of listening effectively to grow her business. An American woman based in Asia ran a small, family-owned graphic design and map company. Because the maps industry is so cyclical (up during tourist season, down the rest of the year), she tried to figure out ways to avoid the financial rollercoaster that came with the nature of her business. One day, some of her clients complained that most name cards, which are so important in Asia, were unattractive. They wished there were exciting and interesting name card design they could use. The business owner took the bull by the horns and began to develop and offer a series of attractive, eye-catching name cards for her clients. This evened out her business throughout the year and provided her with a steady income stream, even outside of tourist season.

I know a small jewelry store owner who had a shop in the same downtown location for more than 20 years. Slowly, his business began to dry up. He tried changing his inventory, hiring better salespeople, even discounting his products. Nothing worked. He finally decided to interview some of his former customers and discovered that a large percentage of them had changed where they lived, moving to the suburbs in the last few years. Their need for a location closer to their homes was what caused them to go to a different jewelry store. The store owner did what any good SME would do and followed suit, following his customers and moving his store to the suburbs, too. The outcome? His business picked up immediately. It was all about listening to his customers and understanding their Need for him to be in the right location.

#2: Focus ... on Focus Groups

A "focus group" consists of a group of potential or existing customers that you gather together for the sole purpose of asking them specific questions about your brand or your business. Focus groups can unearth a veritable treasure chest of knowledge, along with amazing insights into the minds of customers. Big businesses and consumer goods giants spend hundreds of thousands of dollars on these groups every single year. They hire expensive focus group facilitators, rent fancy one-way mirrored meeting rooms, and fly in marketers and R&D teams from across the country to watch and listen to what customers have to say.

Does it sound valuable but way too expensive? It doesn't have to be! You can get the exact same results for next to nothing.

- Gather your customers or potential customers together, order lunch or late-afternoon snacks, and ask them a series of questions. Ask about your products, your brand, your business, and your image, for example. Encourage them to be completely honest. Let them know you value their point of view and that you are simply interested in their perspective.

- Don't judge! There are no "wrong" answers — just answers that reveal how your customers truly feel about what you offer. They are a great source of knowledge and information about your brand! Treat the information as such.

- Take the opportunity to get creative. For example, a children's toy manufacturer asked parents to bring their kids to a focus group and had the children play with the company's latest toys. They asked the parents questions such as: "What kinds of toys do they like to play with? Are they interacting as much with these toys as they are with their toys at home? Given how your child is playing with this toy right now, how likely would you be to consider purchasing it?"

- If you're a restaurant owner, ask current or potential customers to come in and try some new menu items you're considering. What do they like? What do they dislike? Is it worthy of putting on your menu? If not, ask them what you could change that would encourage them to order it.

- If you find it difficult to get people to agree to become part of a focus group, give them an incentive. This might be a free gift or a coupon for a future purchase. You might even make them part of a special membership group.

Most of the time, people love to be asked their point of view on just about anything. In my own personal experience, I've never had a single person turn me down when I've asked them for an opinion about something. I expect you can anticipate a similar response to your own requests.

#3: Customer Observations — No Binoculars Required

Unlike focus groups, "customer observations" don't involve gathering customers in a specific meeting room or venue. Instead, you actually watch them using your product or service as close as possible to the way they would use it in reality.

Let's say you market a product or service that's used in someone's home. To watch a customer in action, you would actually ask to go to the customer's home and observe them using it.

Now, I know this may sound intrusive — maybe even a bit weird — but big businesses do this all the time. While at Procter & Gamble and Bristol-Myers Squibb, I visited people's homes all around the world to watch them do their laundry, wash their hair, feed their babies, etc. This practice really does give you incredible insight into how your brand is being used and helps you uncover your customers' Needs in their own native environment.

Lots of great ideas for new brands have come from these kinds of customer observations. Example: Marketers at P&G did some "home visits" (as they are often called) for the laundry category. As a result, they discovered that customers generally had four piles of clothes in their laundry rooms: whites, darks, mixed colors, and a mysterious "fourth pile." When the marketers asked what that fourth pile was for, customers explained that was a pile of dry-clean-only clothes that weren't dirty enough to be taken to the dry cleaners yet, but just needed "freshening up." That sparked the idea that eventually became the Dryel brand.

If you sell school supplies, for example, watch teachers and students using either your supplies or a competitor's supplies in the classroom. If you offer graphic design or a customized software service, for example, visit your customer's location to see how well the results of your service are working.

#4: Discover Ethnography

You may not be familiar with this word, but you may very well have been the subject of "ethnographic research" at some point in your life.

Just like a "customer observation," ethnography involves observing people who are actually using your product or service. The difference with ethnography is that customers *don't know they're being observed.*

Let's say you get invited to a bar for a special night when they're offering great beers at a discount. The bartender asks you which beer you'd like, and you respond, "Carlsberg." A few minutes later, you're kicked back and relaxed, enjoying your nice, cold beer, when someone saunters up to you, starts a casual chat and, at some point during the conversation, says, "So, you're a Carlsberg fan, eh?" That person may very well be a researcher who is mentally recording your responses. In fact, there might be people located throughout the bar who are watching and informally interviewing bar patrons about what they think of different types of beers. This is done so casually that you might not even recognize you're being interviewed. That's ethnography.

How could you use ethnography to understand the deeper Needs and concerns of *your* customers? If your Target Group is easily identified by the way they look, what they do, or the places they visit, put yourself where you can find them. Then, find a natural way to ask them some questions. They might even be using a competitor's product, which can give you a lot of insight about how to improve your own brand.

When I was responsible for marketing infant formulas, I visited grocery stores and stood with my grocery basket in the baby aisle. I'd watch as mothers walked up to the infant formula shelf and decided which brand to buy. Sometimes, they chose quickly, and other times, they stood there for several minutes reading labels. Once they had made their final decision, I politely asked them if they would mind my asking a few questions about their choice. What a wealth of knowledge I uncovered! Because I had watched them in advance, I knew which mothers were cautious, which mothers had a clear brand choice, which ones were comparing, which particular brands they were considering, etc. That led to a number of insights that influenced, for example, what information to put on our own packaging and what information mothers didn't care about.

The people who founded Groovy Maps did something similar with "man on the street" interviews. They positioned themselves in areas of major cities and waited for tourists to stop and pull out maps. They then approached the tourists and asked, "Could I help you find something?" They offered helpful assistance, and at the end, also queried, "By the way, what do you like about this map? What don't you like about it? What's hard to find? What could have been better about this map?" What a great way, on the spot, to find out more about customer Needs!

How could you do the same with your product or service? Intercept prospects, new customers, and returning buyers alike, and ask them about their current Needs. People are generally happy to tell you what they need because they hope someone like you will come along to fill those Needs!

What if you're thinking of opening a small retail outlet in a local mall, for example? Place yourself in the location you're considering, and watch exactly how many customers walk by. You can make note of whether these customers seem consistent with your Target Group.

Stop and ask passersby how they feel about having your particular type of outlet in this location. It's a fantastic way to determine if your plan is a good one, and it doesn't cost anything but your time. (Strapped for time? Enlist some local college students to do this for you for Marketing class credits.)

#5: Put Your Salespeople on the "Front Line"

When I worked at Mead Johnson Nutritionals, we received approval from headquarters for a very large and expensive research project which would help us uncover new trends and Needs of doctors who treated children and infants. This research, which was planned across an entire region, would be used to fuel our future strategic planning. We had hired a large regional research agency to develop a list of questions to ask physicians, we had identified the specific doctors that the researchers would interview across multiple countries, and we were fully ready to go forth and obtain this invaluable data.

Two days before we were scheduled to start our research, the news came in from HQ: The budget had been cut. Our hearts sank. We were counting on this critical information to build our future brand development plans. Panic began to set in.

We started brainstorming any and all alternatives to get the information. Suddenly, a brilliant idea came to mind. What if we leveraged the same people who were in touch with those same doctors every single day — our local sales teams?

We gathered the list of questions the research agency had developed and e-mailed it to the heads of sales in each country. We shared our situation with them and informed them of the interview dates with doctors that had already been scheduled by the research agency. We then asked specific sales members if they would please show up at the doctor's offices at the designated times and conduct the interviews using the list of questions, recording their answers as they went along. We hung up the phone, took a deep breath, and waited to see what would happen.

Well, the outcome was nothing short of miraculous! Not only did we get incredible insights and groundbreaking information about new customer Needs, but we got daily calls from members of the sales force, all saying the same thing: "Thank you!" Salesperson after salesperson called to tell us that asking the doctors meaningful questions had been an incredible way to deepen their relationships with the very physicians they called on every single day. While the salespeople normally only got one to two minutes of the doctors' time on any given day, the physicians were actually *happy* to talk about what they and their patients needed. The doctors extended the time they had reserved for the interview so that they could share their points of view on the topics that were important to them.

So, if you have a sales force, don't forget that they're already out there interacting with customers day in and day out. Don't underestimate the power of that daily interaction. Recognize that every interaction with a customer is a chance to uncover new client Needs and build your brand in the meantime.

#6: Encourage Your Customers to Complain

Yes, that's right! You *want* complaints. They're truly like gold and are an often overlooked way to build your company's brand. It may sound counter-intuitive, but like author Zig Ziglar said: "Statistics suggest that when customers complain, business owners and managers ought to get excited about it. The complaining customer represents a huge opportunity for more business." Bill Gates agrees: "Your most unhappy customers are your greatest source of learning."

You may not *like* asking for customer complaints because it can sting. But the best brands recognize that they not only want their customers to complain, they *need* that information. It's one of the best ways to find out how to make your services or products better, strengthening your brand and growing your business in the process.

Remember: Positioning is all about how your Target Group perceives, thinks, and feels about your brand, so what better way to find out what needs improvement than listening to complaints from your customers?

The key is: You have to ask. Most customers, unless specifically requested to share feedback, will just keep their complaints to themselves while you scurry around, oblivious, trying to figure out why your revenues are dropping. Actually, worse than that, if your customers aren't complaining *to* you, you can rest assured that they are complaining *about* you. That's the fast-track way to busting your brand, and you definitely don't want that to happen.

- **Ask for feedback** at the end of every engagement or interaction with a customer. It doesn't matter whether you're a CPA or a manufacturer of kitchen cabinets. Whatever your product or service, sit down with your customers to ask what went well and what did not. Bear in mind that customers are more likely to give you feedback on what didn't go well if you let them first tell you what did go well. Make sure you discuss this with them as quickly as possible after they've interacted with your brand. You want the experience to be fresh and clear in their minds.

- **Make it easy for your customers to complain.** I know of one hotel manager who has a policy that at least one key staff member has to stand in the lobby by the exit door from 10:00 a.m. to 12:00 noon every day. Why? Because that's when most guests check out, and it's an opportunity for them to speak to customers about what they enjoyed about their stay and what they didn't enjoy. Someone is right there to ask departing guests questions at the most convenient time.

- **Create print or online forms.** Subway sandwich restaurants have a different strategy to help customers complain easily. When you're checking out, there's a feedback form in plain sight that customers can fill out right away. Customers can also go online and give feedback to any of Subway's 35,000 restaurants in more than 95 countries. How's that for making it easy?

- **Think of all the possible ways your customers might want to complain to you.** By phone? Via e-mail? Via postcard or comment card? Via your website? Use every possible outlet to make it simple for customers to tell you what they think, and make it easy for them to find these outlets. If they have to search for your complaint form on your website, guess what? You've just created another complaint!

- **Always answer customer calls.** You don't necessarily have to have a customer service representative available 24/7, 365 days of the year, but if you don't, set up a dedicated complaint voicemail system. Assign a specific team member or members the task of checking the voicemail messages regularly, and take care of the complaints immediately. Never make the customer wait for a response, and do everything you can to address the customer's concerns right away. If you go that extra mile, you're more likely to have a loyal customer for life.

- **Handle problems immediately and with care.** Once at my company, we received a complaint from a customer who tried to buy an e-book online but was unable to download it. He was clearly upset, so we responded right away and e-mailed him the product directly. On top of that, we sent him an extra gift to say we were sorry for any inconvenience. Afterward, he wrote to us saying that he was not only happy with the response, but that he had recommended our book to four other people! That's the kind of loyalty you want to cultivate.

- **Have a clear and specific written process** to follow for anyone on your team who handles customer complaints. It may sound time-consuming and tedious, but once you have a system in place, you'll be glad you did. Most importantly, make sure your staff handles complaints in a way that is consistent with your Brand Character. Remind your staff that they represent the company's brand and that how they talk to customers — whether in person, on the phone, or in writing — is fundamental to success.

- **Keep track of complaints.** Designate someone to write down complaints and watch for trends. One or two mistakes may not point to a need to change, but consistent issues definitely do. Review the complaints monthly or quarterly (monthly is better if you get a fair number of complaints), and figure out what changes you need to make to your products or services based on the information.

- **Ask complaining customers what they would like to see** with regard to your brand that they aren't seeing now. You may discover new and unmet Needs. Read between the lines. Address the complaints, but go even further if you can. The more your brand meets the Needs of your customers — even the Needs your customers may not yet know they have — the stronger your brand will become.

I know of a lawn care services company that began to notice an increasing number of complaints. When they sat down and assessed the comments, they discovered that their service employees were showing up at customers' homes and treating lawns without warning, and this disturbed the inhabitants of one particular neighborhood where there were a lot of older residents. So, the company changed its policy and required employees not only to call in advance and leave a message letting the customer know when they were coming, but also to ring doorbells upon arrival to let customers know they had arrived. This cut down on complaints, improved the company's relationships with its customers, and strengthened the lawn service's brand along the way.

Get Price Off the Table

Do your customers tell you that what they "need" is a lower price? If so, don't believe it!

Branding Myth:
The only way to be competitive is to lower your price.

Witness the busting of yet another important branding myth! Great brand builders know how to get price off the table by emphasizing the brand Benefits they offer and how well they respond to their customers' Needs. Doing this powerfully is what ends up making price a non-issue.

Good branding is about creating "value," which I like to define as the perceived balance between price and performance. If you, as a customer, want to buy a product or service with a high performance level, you're happy to pay more for it, right? In fact, you probably expect it. If the performance is high and the Benefits are great, you will still consider it a good value. So, you can command a higher price if your customers believe your brand's Benefits are worth it.

One way to increase the perceived value of your brand is to include "freebies." Here are a few examples:

- Some hotels offer free breakfast with every hotel room to automatically increase the perceived value of the room.

- A beauty salon in a Midwestern U.S. state offers a free five-minute scalp massage with every haircut, increasing the perceived value of their service.

- Some online companies offer a free downloadable e-book or report along with every product or service sold via the Internet. Leveraging these kinds of free electronic giveaways also works very well with social media outlets like Facebook and Twitter.

- An accountant who specializes in tax preparation for middle income earners wrote a short booklet of tips to help clients increase their tax savings all year long. He gives it to existing clients for free, which keeps his name in front of his customers. When tax season rolls around, his tax preparation service is the name they remember.

- I know an author who lists many different URLs inside of his book where his readers can access free downloads. They have to purchase the book to gain access to the downloads, but this offer increases the perceived value of his books, even though there is very little cost involved.

Get To It!

So, who says you need to hire a market research firm? You're now armed with an arsenal of low-cost and no-cost ideas for finding out exactly what your customers need from you, and you and your team can carry them out yourself without a great deal of effort. Start with one strategy and branch out from there. You'll soon find that your customers are a veritable gold mine of information for building your brand now that you have some great tips for getting the information you need from them.

Remember: Your company would no longer exist if it weren't for your customers. As Amazon.com founder Jeff Bezos put it: "We see our customers as invited guests to a party, and we are the hosts. It's our job every day to make every important aspect of the customer experience a little bit better."

14

HIDDEN DIAMONDS IN THE ROUGH

Brand-Building Asset #2 — Customers: The Value of *Existing* Customers

"In marketing, I've seen only one strategy that can't miss — and that is to market to your best customers first, your best prospects second, and the rest of the world last."
— JOHN ROMERO, VIDEO GAME INDUSTRY ENTREPRENEUR

THERE'S AN OLD SAYING that new friends are silver, while old friends are gold. In business, these "old friends" are your existing customers. Just how golden are they? Studies show that it can cost as much as six to nine times more to attract and keep a new customer than it costs to keep an existing customer happy.

Think about how that could impact your bottom line. If you have $100 to spend on marketing, would you rather spend it on a customer who already believes in you, has had a positive experience with your brand, and who is highly likely to use your products or services again? Or would you rather spend $600 to $900 to *possibly* win over a new customer who *may or may not* like your brand and may never buy? The choice is clear.

Existing customers are low-hanging fruit when it comes to brand building. Don't get me wrong — it's important to continue to grow your business with new prospects. But in the process, far too many business owners forget to nurture relationships with existing customers. So, get feedback from them. Find out who they are, what they need, what about your brand works for them, and what they'd like you to improve.

How do you do that? Establish ongoing, two-way communications. No one wants to be "talked at," but nine times out of ten, clients will welcome a conversation. Let's explore some ways that you can talk "with" your existing customer base and build a powerhouse brand in the process.

Open a Dialogue

Creating newsletters and blogs are excellent, low-cost ways to open communication with your current customers. Blogs are online, of course, and newsletters can be e-mailed in low-cost digital form. Or you can snail mail them in print form (a little more costly). Not sure in which format(s) your customers would like to receive information from you? Conduct a simple survey to find out. (Keep in mind that a brief survey is yet another touch point with your customers — one that shows you care about each customer's point of view.)

But remember: A successful newsletter or blog isn't a sales document! It's called a "news" letter for a reason. It's all about adding value and sharing information. It sets you up as an expert and keeps your name in front of your customers on a regular basis. So, make sure it includes tips, data, and other information that will be truly useful to your customers. If what you share in your communications is useless or all about promoting you and your brand, it will become an annoyance, and recipients will hit the "delete" button as fast as they receive it.

Don't get me wrong — it's okay to have a little bit of information about your business in your newsletters. Just try to keep it "newsy" with an announcement about a new product or service, a blurb about a new industry affiliation, or perhaps an article about a new or veteran employee that highlights your company's expertise. I recommend a 3:1 ratio in your newsletters — three pieces of useful information for every one piece of news about your business.

As with any marketing materials, the key is to make sure that your newsletter is consistent with what your brand stands for and with the Brand Character you want to own. If you run a highly unique furniture store that carries quirky, unusual, avant-garde inventory, make sure your newsletter and blog reflects this "quirkiness" as well. For example, you might include slanted pictures and unusual colors mixed together. If you want your brand of shoe store to come across as relaxed, comfortable, and laid-back, even your choice of font will impact your brand image. (Don't believe me? Type the exact same phrase in Comic

Sans font and again in Times New Roman, compare them side-by-side, and see how different the phrase "feels" when you read them!)

Maybe you think you're not a great writer? You can outsource any and all writing work at surprisingly low cost. Check out online writer "brokerage" services like Elance.com and Guru.com for freelance writers who offer their services to SMEs and solo-preneurs.

Here are some tips for making your newsletter the type that customers actually look forward to receiving, rather than dread:

- Do your homework. If you don't know your existing customers well, you won't be clear on what they want from your newsletter. Let your first newsletter be a type of online input gatherer, asking clients what type of information would be most helpful for them. Give them a nice incentive to participate, such as a free downloadable industry report or a small digital booklet that contains valuable information.

- Once you have a good idea of what your customers would like to see in communications from you, use your newsletter as an opportunity to get to know your clients even better, discovering their new and changing Needs more quickly. Ask readers to answer questions you'd like to know about, such as: "On a scale of 1-10, how helpful have our newsletters been, and why?" or "What past blog posts have you found most helpful?" Let them know their opinions count. In that same vein, include a link in your newsletter to your blog where clients can "sound off" and share their own points of view on your topics.

- Make it easy for customers to answer your questions quickly by allowing them to click "yes" or "no" answers. SurveyMonkey.com is an extremely easy and low-cost way to create a digital poll. I use this service often; in fact, while trying to decide between various subtitles for this book, we asked hundreds of SME owners and solo-preneur customers to complete a simple online mini-survey. We made it easy to participate quickly, customers were happy to lend their points of view, and we ended up with a subtitle that we were sure would appeal to SMEs and solo-preneurs.

- Keep your customers entertained and engaged with fun questions, polls, and sweepstakes. One business owner I know has a "read to the bottom of the newsletter" club where he asks his readers to answer a question based on something that was written in one of the articles. A correct answer gains them entry in a monthly raffle for prizes. It's engaging, and his customers are sure to read his entire newsletter!

- At the bottom of your newsletter and blog, include a "forward" button to invite customers to share the information with others who might benefit. This is a quick, easy — and free! — way to get an instant referral, and it only requires a couple of mouse clicks on the part of your customer.

- My own company, Brand Development Associates International, has published a newsletter for a few years now. I love it when I ask a new customer how they found us, and they respond, "Through your newsletter!" The cost of a newsletter and/or blog is low, but the impact on your brand and your business can be incredibly high.

- A word of caution, however: We're careful not to inundate our customers with weekly newsletters. We only send a newsletter or post a blog when we feel we have something worthy of sharing. Many of our clients have told us they appreciate that. In fact, according to our online statistics, we have one of the lowest newsletter dropout rates in our industry. So, be careful not to "overdo" it, as it will have a negative impact on your brand. Although many would argue differently, I really believe quality is more important than quantity. Guard against your brand becoming like your old Aunt Frieda who just can't seem to stop talking. Eventually, you just quit calling or visiting her. That's the last thing you want your customers to do!

- If the idea of sending out a regular newsletter makes you want to hide under the covers, try sending out low-cost postcards once in a while instead. A professional speaker colleague of mine, Scott, does this on a regular basis. To help solidify his position as a motivational humorist, he creates and sends funny postcards to his customers, usually around specific holidays. For example, on Halloween, he might send a postcard that lists "10 Scary Thoughts to Ponder for Halloween," filled with ideas like:
  - I went to buy some camouflage trousers the other day, but I couldn't find any.

- Reading while sunbathing makes you well-red.
- What's the definition of a will? (It's a dead giveaway.)
- If you don't pay your exorcist, you get repossessed.
- There are three kinds of people: those who can count and those who can't.

Scott's quirky sense of humor comes through and helps him stay on the minds of his customers. In fact, some of Scott's clients have even framed his postcards! Can you imagine your marketing materials becoming art for *your* customers' walls?

- The unstoppable rise of social media has made it easier than ever for small businesses and solo-preneurs alike to get a back-and-forth dialogue going with their customers. You can tweet information about a new product and ask questions of your customers that they can answer very quickly. You can easily post a poll on Facebook that customers can participate in with a simple click. And it doesn't have to cost you a thing!

The bottom line is: Thanks to the advent of social media, there has never been a better time to communicate your brand in low-cost or no-cost ways.

Don't Hesitate to Blow Your Own Horn

Do your existing customers only benefit from using *one* of the products or services you offer? Do your customers even *know* what else you offer? Do you have other talents or skills that you haven't bothered to tell your clients about?

This is one of the simplest, lowest-cost, yet overlooked, ways of growing your business and strengthening your brand: Make sure your customers know about the full range of products and services you offer.

- If you've been a consultant for a particular company for a while, let executives at that company know you also work with clients as a one-on-one coach.

- Maybe you're a dentist who has just filled a cavity for someone who has slightly yellowed teeth. Let this patient know about your teeth-whitening products and services.

- If you're an author, and someone asks to publish one of your articles on a website with a lot of traffic, let them know you are open to writing a monthly column for them.

If your customers don't know the full range of all you have to offer, you've missed a great opportunity to generate more business and build a stronger brand name at the same time.

I know of a local, family-run greeting card company that recently sent a postcard to all of their existing customers announcing a new set of card designs they were launching. The bottom of that postcard included a small section highlighting the other products they offer, including gift tags, gift wrap, coffee mugs, wedding invitations, moving announcements, and coloring books. Until I received that postcard, I had no idea the company offered all of those products!

How could you let your customers know the range of other services or products you offer?

Business (Sometimes) Means Having to Say You're Sorry…

It happened! You or a member of your team made a colossal mistake, and your customer is furious.

Face it: As a business, you're bound to make mistakes. It's what you do about it that matters most when it comes to brand building. In fact, the key to success is changing whatever happened from a brand "buster" to a brand "booster." How? Apologize in a meaningful and strategic way.

I experienced this myself as a customer. As background, keep in mind that I travel extensively — to the tune of about 300,000 miles per year (go frequent flyer miles!) — and the majority of that travel is international. Late one night, I flew into Kuala Lumpur, Malaysia, arriving at my hotel at about midnight. As you can imagine, I was exhausted after a long day. I also needed to get to sleep as quickly as possible so that I could be up and ready to present at a meeting at 8:00 the next morning. Standing at the hotel reception counter, I heard the words that are enough to make any traveler's hair stand on end: "We're very sorry, Ms. Bence, but we have no reservation under your name, and our hotel is fully booked."

As you can imagine, I was not a happy camper! There I was in a foreign country with no place to sleep and no easy alternatives. In the end, that hotel sent me to another hotel, and I did finally get a room. However, I didn't get to sleep until about 1:30 a.m., so I was anything but "fresh and ready" for my presentation the next morning.

I sent an e-mail to my travel agent asking her what happened. This agent responded in a way that I will never forget.

- She immediately contacted my executive assistant and made sure I was well taken care of during the remainder of my stay in Malaysia.

- She arranged for me to get a VIP entrance into Thailand, the country where I was heading next. There, someone met me at the gate and zipped me through the airport in one of those annoying little cars, making sure I got through immigration quickly. (Actually, those little cars are only annoying if you're walking; they're a lot of fun when you're riding in one of them!)

- When I arrived back at my office, there was a *handwritten* letter waiting for me from the president of the travel agency, apologizing personally for my inconvenience.

- They also purchased a very nice travel bag for me to help "make my next trip a little easier."

Now, *that's* an apology! Everything they did to respond to their error was personalized and related to making my current and future trips as easy and enjoyable as possible. You can bet I continued to do business with this travel agency, despite their big mistake.

Stop for a moment and think right now: What could you do, strategically, that could make a difference in terms of how your customers feel about your brand even when someone in your company makes a colossal mistake? Whatever you do, make sure it ties into your brand's Benefits that you want to instill in your customers' minds.

Give It the Personal Touch

Just like my travel agent responded in a very personal way, recognizing and rewarding your existing customers in a personal way also allows you to deepen your relationship with them and solidify their loyalty to your brand. Let's look at several ways you can do this.

Send a Note. Send your existing customers a handwritten thank-you note for no other reason than just to say you value their business and appreciate their loyalty. How would you feel if you received something like that in the mail? Clients have told me they really appreciate that personal touch.

Remember Them. As you learn details about the personal lives of your customers and their businesses, keep track of the information. Some companies spend thousands of dollars on customer relations management (CRM) software, but you don't have to do that. Save money and headaches by simply adding the information to your Microsoft Outlook program or by developing an Excel spreadsheet with the information organized by customer name. Review the details before your next meeting with a customer, and ask questions related to what you've written down. Your customers will be impressed that you remembered. And even if you didn't remember everything by heart, you took the time to write it down so that you could bring it up again. Don't you appreciate it when someone does that for you? It's a strong brand booster.

Be Welcoming. Always provide customers with a warm welcome when they come to your offices, and brief your receptionist about who is coming so that he/she knows everyone by name. The Gansevoort Hotel in New York City, for example, embroiders the initials of each guest on a pillow case before they arrive. Of course, you don't need to be nearly as extravagant — or spend nearly as much money — to make your customers feel welcome. I once visited a potential business partner's office and walked in to see a sign that said, "Welcome, Brenda Bence." It made me feel special. This kind of attention to customers doesn't cost much, but it pays off in volumes because it makes a great connection that boosts your relationship with your customer, and thus, strengthens your brand.

Invite Customers to Events. Include customers in company events like golf tournaments or conferences that you organize or attend. If you're going to an event and can only invite one or two people, ask your biggest clients.

If you can afford it, host a client appreciation party. Even this can be done inexpensively with a little bit of ingenuity. For example, hold an outdoor potluck picnic for your customers, and invite their families to come along.

Pssst! Pass the Word

We all love to get referrals from our customers and colleagues, but if you're just waiting for them to fall into your lap, you may be waiting a while. Here are some simple, low-cost tips to help you get more referrals:

You Have to Ask! If you aren't asking your existing customers regularly for referrals, you're missing a truly golden opportunity to build your brand. How often do you say something like, "By the way, could you give me the names of three other people who might benefit from our services?" In my own experience, that simple five seconds of my time has turned into business again and again. People are usually genuinely happy to help you, especially if you consistently provide them with good services or quality products. The thing is: As business people, we simply don't ask often enough.

If asking your customers for referrals makes you shake in your shoes, simply get comfortable saying something less direct like, "I'm never too busy to talk with your friends or colleagues" or "I'd be happy to take you and your friends/colleagues out to lunch sometime so that we can talk about how I might be able to help them as well." The key is to find the wording that's most natural for you. Then, make asking for referrals a regular habit.

You could even frame a notice at your store or office that asks politely for referrals. A sign on the wall of my doctor's office says, "The greatest compliment you can give us is a referral to your family and friends." Heck, I know a real estate agent who put that phrase on the back of her business card! What a great way to remind people that you appreciate referrals.

Timing and Details. The key to getting the best brand-building referrals is to be specific and to strike while the iron is hot. Let's say that I've just performed a service for a client and have asked for feedback (we will talk more about this during the Products and Services chapter coming up). Once I've listened carefully, the next step I take is to ask for a referral. Most of the time, clients will give me names and phone numbers right there on the spot. Make sure you not only get names and phone numbers, but e-mail and website addresses, too, if you can. The devil is in the details!

When I conduct a workshop, I always include a section at the end of my feedback form that asks: "Would you recommend this program to your friends or colleagues? If yes, please list the names and phone numbers of five people you think would benefit from attending this same kind of training." This allows my staff to follow up with those individuals, and we can say, "Your colleague, _____, thought that you would enjoy attending our upcoming workshop, so he passed your name on to us." At a minimum, we ask permission to add those individuals' names and contact information to our mailing list and notify them when the next workshop is coming up.

Let No Referral Go Unappreciated. When a customer refers business to you, offer a reward of some kind. Sometimes, a simple call to say "thank you" is appropriate, but something like a handwritten thank-you note, flowers, or a bottle of wine will encourage more referrals. If you're a dentist, for example, you might give customers who refer business to you a nice electric toothbrush. If you're a hair stylist, give referring customers your latest hair product in a nice gift bag. A private health club might offer a two-month membership extension as a thank you. When I was responsible for hiring vendors during my last corporate job, I referred a supplier to someone, and he got the job. As a thank you, he gave me a beautiful globe paperweight. It sits on my desk, reminding me of this supplier every time I look at it. As a result, I've referred business to him again and again.

Yes, these kinds of gifts may cost you a bit of money, but when you think of the cost as a percentage of the incremental revenues coming in, it's minor. You'll be pleasantly surprised how making this a regular practice can result in a booming referral business and the rapid growth of your brand.

Finder's Fees. Another type of thank-you gift is a finder's fee. For example, if I refer business to my web designer, I get 10% of the revenues that come from that new business. Of course, you want to let customers and contacts know that you offer this kind of arrangement. When you meet someone for the first time at a networking event or elsewhere, if you feel the person might be good to work with, mention your finder's fee arrangement when you talk about your business. The key is to make sure this person understands the nature of your brand and the kinds of customers you're targeting.

You can develop an affiliate program on your website, too, so that your customers can earn money through giving you online referrals. It's simple, it doesn't cost you anything, it builds your brand, and let's face it: Who doesn't like to make money in their jammies?

Reciprocate. Don't forget to look for opportunities to refer business to *your* customers and strategic alliance partners, too. If I help customers build their businesses, they are more likely to help me build my brand in return. It's the old adage at work: "I scratch your back; you scratch mine."

The bottom line? Never forget that a happy customer is your very best brand cheerleader and that your existing customers are also your most profitable ones. The more reasons you give them to become enthusiastic about your brand and what you offer, the more loyal they will remain, the more referrals you'll get in return, and the faster you'll grow your brand.

15

DEVELOP A SUPERIORITY COMPLEX

Brand-Building Asset #3 — Your Products and Services

"No matter what your product is, you are ultimately in the education business. Your customers need to be constantly educated about the many advantages of doing business with you, trained to use your products more effectively, and taught how to make never-ending improvement in their lives."

— ROBERT G. ALLEN, AUTHOR

WHAT IS THE THIRD ASSET YOU ALREADY HAVE that can help you build a terrific brand? Your very own products and services. This may come as a surprise, and you may be wondering how that works. There are many ways we'll outline in this chapter, but first and foremost, you must leverage your products and services to differentiate your brand in the marketplace.

If you're one of the lucky ones with products or services that are clearly better than your competition, celebrate! And please don't keep it to yourself — flaunt it! You'll learn ways to do just that in this chapter.

On the other hand, if you're like most SME owners and solo-preneurs I know, you may be thinking, "Actually, Brenda, if I'm honest with myself, my products and services are similar to my competitors." If that rings true for you, don't worry. You'll learn a host of ways to take a parity-performing product or service and make it superior in the minds of your customers.

Superiority Doesn't Equal Dishonesty

The first—and most important—step to take when considering how your products and services can serve your brand is to be truly honest with yourself about their strengths and weaknesses. There's nothing worse in branding than a lot of bravado with no legitimate product or service to back it up. You know what I'm talking about—you've seen it again and again in bad marketing. Maybe it's an ad for a drug that claims just two pills are equal to six competitor's pills or an instant weight loss product that promises you'll lose 20 pounds in two weeks. As a lifelong brander and marketer, that kind of advertising makes my skin crawl.

Don't let that be you! In order to build a powerhouse brand, you absolutely must take a good hard look at your offerings and objectively review the strengths and the weaknesses of your products and services. Be as unbiased as you can, and if you need to find someone else who can give you an honest, straightforward opinion, do it. This is a critical foundation to building an authentic, lasting brand.

Give It Away

Once you've done your assessment, if you really do have products and services with noticeable superiority, get them in the hands of your Target Group—even if you have to give them away for free. That's right. If what you offer is truly superior—and that superiority is noticeable in one use or one experience—those customers will continue to buy and will tell all of their friends about you, guaranteed.

I once attended a networking event at a newly opened spa with the sole intention of having a kick-back evening. The truth is: I'm not much of a spa person, but they wanted to attract people they thought might be potential customers. So I went, expecting nothing more than a nice time catching up with some friends.

Upon arrival, everyone put their business cards into a fish bowl for a raffle, and at the end of the night, guess who won the free one-hour spa treatment? That's right—yours truly. They gave me a certificate, everyone applauded, and my photo was taken.

Time passed, and I completely forgot about the certificate. About a week before its expiration date, my assistant came into my office and said, "Brenda, don't forget to sign up for your free one-hour spa treatment." She made an appointment for me, and I showed up at the spa a couple of days later.

Now, frankly, I was a bit reluctant to go. Again, I'm not really a spa person, and with traffic, it was going to take a much-needed couple of hours out of my busy week. But I figured I might as well take advantage of the free gift.

Then, I walked into the spa, and my attitude changed dramatically! That experience was unlike any other I have ever had. The comfy slippers, the plush robe, the soothing music, the quiet and luxurious ambience, the aromatherapy, the experienced professional masseuse...all were nothing short of spectacular. I loved every minute of it! And not only did I tell dozens of friends about that positive experience, but I ended up going back there three more times — and I paid a very hefty price to do so.

This story drives home a smart branding principle used cleverly by that spa: They knew they offered a superior product and experience, and they knew it would pay off to offer it for free to someone in their Target Group.

In my own business, I do the same thing by providing a complimentary coaching session to people I meet if I think they fit my Target Group. The truth is: I know I provide a superior coaching program, so I don't mind offering a trial session for free. And it has paid off. In fact, more than 90% of the people who come to me for a trial session sign up for a full-term coaching program.

Do *you* have a superior performing service or product? If so, how could you get your customers to experience it firsthand? It's a powerful way to build your brand.

Creating a "Meaningful Point of Difference"

I keep a funny cartoon by my desk that shows a picture of a young boy with a lemonade stand that sports the sign: "25 cents for lemonade. Comes with free Wi-Fi."

That cartoon taps into yet another powerful branding strategy: If you *don't* have noticeable superiority, or if your superiority is hard to prove (let's face it: lemonade is lemonade, right?), then *create* a meaningful point of difference that will help your brand stand out from the rest. Just as the little boy in the cartoon offered something unique and different to make his product a superior choice vs. competing lemonade stands, you can do the same. Once you start looking around, you'll find there are many ways to set your brand apart from your competition.

Take "Double A," a brand of copier paper. Most people believe "copy paper is copy paper," wouldn't you agree? So, how on earth do you differentiate yourself in an industry like that? Well, when the green movement came along, Double A decided to emphasize the fact that its paper comes from farmed trees, so it appeals to the emotional Need of its Target Group to take care of the environment and contribute to building a better planet through what they buy. It has helped Double A create a nice, meaningful point of difference for what is otherwise seen as a commodity product.

Here's an example from my own experience: One Sunday morning, I woke up early, walked into my living room and, to my horror, discovered a water pipe had burst overnight! Our hardwood floor was flooded, and all of my imported rugs were "floating" on about two inches of H_2O! Among the first things I did was call Raj, the carpet shop owner who had sold me the rugs several years before. I asked him if there was anything he could do, and even though it was a Sunday morning, Raj rushed over immediately with a truck. He gathered up all of the wet, sopping rugs and promised to bring them back in great condition. To be perfectly honest, I was doubtful.

A week and a half later, Raj showed up at my doorstep with the rugs — in picture perfect shape and looking like new. What a relief!

As Raj and his team brought our rugs inside, I noticed they had also brought several other rugs.

"What are those for?" I asked.

"Well, I noticed when I was here before that you had some spaces on your floor where a few more rugs might be nice," he answered with a genuine smile. He explained that there was no obligation; I could simply hold onto the rugs and "try them out" for a couple of weeks.

I didn't believe we needed any more rugs, but the man had just prevented us from losing thousands of dollars in destroyed rugs. So, I politely agreed to keep the "trial rugs" for a couple of weeks.

Of course, you can probably guess what happened. We became so accustomed to those new rugs during the following two weeks that we ended up buying six more! Raj was right about our home needing more rugs, and they *did* look great in our place. But even more importantly, Raj had been speedy, effective, and polite, and he really took the time to understand what I needed from him. It wasn't that he necessarily had a superior product. I know of other carpets that are equally as nice. But Raj's super service and attention made him stand out, and that's what drove our loyalty to his brand.

Just like those rugs, the goal is to get your customers so accustomed to your brand that they just can't live without it. Do what it takes to make your brand irresistible to them. The Charles Hotel in Boston is an example of this within the hospitality industry. To stand out among the other high-end hotels with which it competes, it created an exceptional point of difference by being pet-friendly, offering its guests' canine companions a water bowl and treats, and allowing pets to stay in rooms. This makes a tremendous difference to a friend of mine who's a devoted dog owner. When she travels to Boston, you can bet she never stays at any other hotel but The Charles.

What kinds of irresistible hooks for your brand can you create that will stand out with your customers and drive brand loyalty?

Six Elements to Superiority

Another way to drive perceived superiority for your brand is to go back to the six elements of your Brand Positioning Statement:

- Target Group
- Needs
- Competitive Framework
- Benefits
- Reasons Why
- Brand Character

Each one of those elements, masterfully managed, can help your customers see your brand in a unique and different way, creating perceived superiority even if your product or service isn't necessarily better than your competitors. Here are a few examples of brands that have done this successfully.

Target Group:

- The soda 7-Up was positioned as the "uncola" for years, appealing to people who think against the grain and want something other than the sodas most of the world drinks.

- Hay House, the publishing company started by Louise Hay, the author of *You Can Heal Your Life,* focuses on the niche market of people who are passionate about personal and spiritual development.

- WeTransfer.com targets people who want to be able to e-mail extremely large files for free via the Internet.

Needs:

- Remember how Starbucks uncovered an emotional Need? This emotional Need has made its customers actually perceive it as superior, even though many would argue that Starbucks' coffee is equal in taste to others.

- Thailand's Bumrungrad Hospital fills a very specific service Need that is growing by leaps and bounds — medical tourism. To international customers across the globe, it offers the unique opportunity to come to tropical Thailand for elective surgical procedures while also enjoying a great holiday during the recovery period. In this way, Bumrungrad fills both the functional and emotional Needs of its Target Group. And even if its surgery offerings are similar to other hospitals, it comes across as a superior choice in the eyes of its patients.

Competitive Framework:

- McDonald's differentiates itself by making its establishments not just fast food restaurants like its competitors, but places where families could go for *fun* as well as food. This meant that McDonald's no longer competed only with KFC or Burger King, but with other fun family places like zoos and amusement parks.

- As I mentioned in a previous chapter, Santa Fe moving company has beaten the competition by becoming a "relocation service specialist" — far more than just a "mover." Now, it's a one-stop shop for all that's required when a family moves, from setting up telephone service, to hiring domestic staff, to finding schools for children. By doing so, it has created a superior brand in the hearts and minds of its customers.

Benefits:

- Volvo has focused on safety as its core Benefit, and that focus has helped the company to create a point of differentiation for everything it does, making Volvo well-known for its safety record all over the world. Remember, too, that safety and the feeling of being safe are both functional and emotional Benefits.

- iPod was one of the first MP3 players to provide the great Benefit of easy mobile entertainment, and it built a massive brand by meeting that previously unmet Need.

- H&R Block differentiates itself by providing the functional Benefit of accurate, inexpensive tax preparation and faster refunds, along with the emotional Benefit of reassurance that your tax return is in an expert's hands.

Reasons Why:

- Dove uses a Reason Why as its point of difference by focusing on the fact that it contains "one-quarter cleansing cream." This well-known and well-advertised Reason Why is what convinces Dove's Target Group that the brand has superior moisturizing properties.

- The Mayo Clinic, one of the world's most celebrated hospitals, has powerful Reasons Why — the combination of top doctors and researchers on staff and state-of-the-art facilities serves to drive home an image of superiority.

Brand Character:

- We already talked about the most obvious examples of brands that use their Brand Character to differentiate them from one another — Coke and Pepsi. Their ingredients are almost identical, but Coke and Pepsi each have their own "personality" created by marketers. This point of difference has created strong loyalty to one brand over the other, creating a sense of superiority in the eyes of their customers.

Now, reflect back on the six elements of your own Brand Positioning Statement. In which of these elements is your brand most unique versus your competition? How could you leverage a meaningful point of difference in your communications with customers to create perceived superiority, turning it into a competitive advantage, and making it ownable and exclusive for your brand?

What's the "Experience" of Your Brand?

Yet another way to create a powerful point of difference is to focus on the *experience* you offer customers with your product or services. Let's consider the coffee industry as an example:

- When coffee is in its bean state — nothing more than just a commodity — the cost is around 1¢ to 2¢ per cup.

- Put the coffee into packaging, add a brand name, and stick it on a grocery store shelf for sale, and the cost of that same coffee rises to 5¢ to 25¢ per cup.

- If you grind and brew that coffee and add in service at a restaurant like Dunkin' Donuts, the cost goes up even more, to around 75¢ to $1.50 per cup.

- And then, there's Starbucks, where we pay a whopping $2.00 to $5.00 per cup. Are we crazy? Is that "choca-mocha-froca" truly that much better? (I can never keep those names straight.) One could argue that it really doesn't matter whether the coffee is better because the main Benefit Starbucks offers is a unique *experience*. As I've said, this sets the brand apart and drives hundreds of thousands of consumers every day to spend exorbitant prices on a cup of coffee.

You can do the same with your brand. Finding ways to improve the *experience* you offer your customers is one of the fastest and least expensive ways to build your brand while raising your prices at the same time. If your brand offers a better experience, trust me — people will pay a higher price for it.

Put Yourself in Your Customers' Shoes

So, what experience do your customers have with *your* brand? Would you want to be your client? If so, why? If not, why not?

If you aren't completely sure about the experience your customers are having with your brand, you need to find out. At a minimum, you should use your own products or services on a regular basis. Experience what your customers are going through, and you'll not only gain a new perspective on the condition of your business and how it operates, but you'll see your products or services — and your brand — with fresh eyes.

Still, of course, it's difficult for you to be truly objective about your own company. How do you get an unbiased viewpoint about your products and services?

One option is to use a "mystery shopper." That's a person who is hired to use your products or experience your services. He or she might make a phone call to your customer service line, eat at your restaurant, drop by your office to make an inquiry, or stay at your hotel for a night. Afterward, the mystery shopper offers you a detailed and unbiased debrief of their experience with regard to the quality of your service or product, and you can use that data to understand the health of your brand.

Big companies spend hundreds of thousands of dollars every year on mystery shoppers because they know it's a powerful way to maintain quality and strengthen their brands. But, here's some good news: You can get the exact same results at low cost or no cost at all! Simply enlist family, friends, or existing customers to "mystery shop" for you. If you want, you can offer a free product, service, or gift in return.

The key is: Your staff should never know that the individual in question is a mystery shopper. They must think of that person as "just" another customer. That's the only way your shopper will receive the exact same experience as your other clients.

If you want, give your mystery shoppers specific instructions as to what you would like them to notice. For example, you might want to know how many rings it takes before someone answers the phone at your company or how long customers have to wait in line. A friend of mine runs a chain of quick-service restaurants that tried mystery shopping. Their order takers had been told to ask each customer, "Would you like fries with that?" but mystery shopping revealed that the order takers weren't asking that question. By reinforcing the importance of making that one simple statement, sales of french fries increased 60%!

How could you use the concept of mystery shopping to better understand the experience of *your* brand through your customers' eyes? What specifics about your products or services would you ask your mystery shoppers to focus on?

Assess the Best and the Worst

After receiving honest feedback through mystery shopping or another means, make an assessment of where you stand: Is your product truly superior, equal, or even inferior to your competitors? If so, in what ways?

- If the benefits you offer through your products or services are truly superior, is that superiority visible and tangible? In other words, can your customers see or experience them immediately? If so, as I mentioned before, get your products or services into the hands of key potential customers — now!

- If your products or services are equal or inferior, how could you make them better? What are the biggest issues that were uncovered, and how can you use that knowledge to make improvements, both in the short-term and in the long-term? The foundation of any brand promise is based on what you deliver through your products and services, so it's fundamental to take the time and effort to get this right.

Creating Credibility

Another way to strengthen the perception of superiority is to create a product or service with the express intention of boosting your credibility.

Create an Award. Agro Food Resources (AFR) is an example of a small company that did just that. AFR is in the business of assuring food safety in restaurants and factories by checking to see if the business is adhering to safety regulations. To strengthen that brand positioning, they ingeniously created the "Best Hygiene Restaurant Award" in partnership with a local magazine. Being the judges for the award, which was publicly announced in the magazine, gave AFR the opportunity to inspect many of the best restaurants, hotels, and bars throughout the city where they operated. As a result, not only did they get more establishments to focus on hygiene, but they got a lot of new business by pointing out to these same companies some of the operational procedures they needed to improve in order to adhere to proper hygiene standards and qualify to win the award.

Become a Publicity Hound. Write about your specialty, and get your articles published in local, regional, or national publications, or on the Internet — whatever your customers read. It's free, and it works. It solidifies your position in the market, strengthens your brand, and gives your potential customers something of value. I know a tax advisor who writes a monthly column for a few newspapers. All it costs him is the time it takes to write, and those publications welcome the content. The articles give him visibility, and it's also a great credibility booster to be able to say he has been quoted in a number of publications. In fact, on a personal level, writing articles has given my own brand a boost, too. In a section of my bio that I send to prospective clients, I say: "Brenda has been featured in more than 300 media outlets and publications all over the world, including NBC-TV, *Reader's Digest*, *Financial Times*, *Smart Money*, and *Entrepreneur*."

Here are four websites that are great places to start if you want to publish articles on the Internet, especially if you want to reach a global audience. They are all highly ranked and receive a lot of traffic:

- EzineArticles.com
- GoArticles.com
- SelfGrowth.com
- IdeaMarketers.com

Write a Book. There's a reason the word "authority" is derived from the word "author."

Take Mike, an American attorney in Bangkok, Thailand, who wanted to find a way to differentiate himself from other attorneys.

He realized there were a limited number of English-language books that explained Thai business law well, so he decided to write his own. The outcome? He became a perceived expert as soon as the book was published! He began to get offers to speak at conferences and, as a result, Michael's practice has grown tremendously. People simply "see" him differently now, and the book was so popular that he wrote two more on related topics that allowed him to expand his expertise beyond the Thai borders. That's how you build a powerful *regional* brand!

By the way, your book doesn't have to be long. Even pulling together a nice booklet of helpful information can differentiate you and your offerings. And if you worry that you don't have much to offer, just think: How could you write about your subject matter expertise from your own unique perspective? After all, no one looks at your topic the same way you do.

These days, with so many easy publishing methods out there, the cost of creating a book is much lower than in the past. For example, start out publishing a digital e-book. It's a less expensive format, and it's growing in popularity.

Leverage Social Media. Create a fan page on Facebook, and include testimonials or links to articles you've written. Follow the example of Mark, a solo-preneur personal trainer who regularly posts videos to promote his service. He also gives away free trials and keeps customers and potential customers aware of events, new products, and new services, all through his Facebook page.

Ask for recommendations through your LinkedIn network, and post videos on YouTube about topics related to your area of expertise. Tweet about trends in your industry or links to articles you've written. Social media provides fast and easy exposure for your brand — at no cost at all — and these sites will help you create a superior brand image.

Don't Scrimp on Your Website and E-mail Address

Let your website be a point of difference for your brand, as well. Look at your competitors' websites objectively, and write down what you like and dislike about them. Then, come back and look at your own website. How does it compare?

You don't have to spend a lot of money on a website, but spend enough to make sure it's something you're proud of. Unlike the old days when not everyone had a website, it's now the price of entry for any business — SMEs and solo-preneurs included. Even if your site doesn't have much "functionality," it's an important touch point with your customers, so make sure it looks professional, is easy to navigate, and perfectly reflects your Brand Character.

Use a domain name that's meaningful and that differentiates your brand from competition. However, don't be overly clever, a branding mistake made by a lot of entrepreneurs. Keep your brand's URL reasonably simple, and make sure it's something your customers are likely to remember. If you're a solo-preneur and haven't done so already, put this book down and go buy your own name as a domain right now! It's a key part of your brand — you need to own it before someone else does.

Once you have your website, here are some tips to make it work hard for you and your brand:

- Update your site whenever you have something meaningful to share, like a new product or service. It keeps your customers informed, and regular updates will keep your site moving up in the search engines.

- Invest time to learn about search engine optimization. Take advantage of the wealth of SEO information available on the Internet for free. Don't want to bother? Go to a local college, and post a "want ad" to hire an IT student. They'll be happy to help you manage your website every once in a while in exchange for a little cash.

- Include testimonials on your site, and make sure your visitors can immediately identify what your business does when they arrive on your home page. Studies show that a visitor will click away from your site within one to three seconds if they can't tell what you do. So, make sure the benefits you offer your customers are highlighted, front and center!

One big mistake many small business owners and solo-preneurs make is to use @gmail.com, @yahoo.com, @aol.com, or @hotmail.com for their e-mail address rather than their own registered domain name. This is a big brand buster! Doing so automatically downgrades you and your business, making you appear unprofessional and, quite frankly, "small potatoes." Use an e-mail address that ends with the domain name of your website. If you want to come across professional and give the impression that your company is larger than it is, use "firstname.lastname@domainname.com" for the e-mail addresses of everyone on your team. If you only use first names, it may come across warm and friendly, but it also gives an impression that you're a small, family organization. (Caveat: For some Target Groups, of course, coming across as a small organization might be an advantage, so make your decision based on your own individual brand circumstances.)

Use your e-mail signature to your benefit. It's yet another effective-yet-zero-cost way to strengthen your brand. A client of mine named John, who is Founder and Executive Director of an international not-for-profit, includes links in his e-mail signature to YouTube videos that highlight his organization's latest projects. One consultant I know includes links to his social media pages as part of his e-mail sign-off. As long as you have excellent quality content at the other end of these links, including them is a great way to brand your business.

And while you're at it, don't forget that you should also include an e-mail signature on your smartphone so that you don't miss an opportunity to pass along information about your brand when you send e-mails remotely.

In addition to the "usuals" of name, title, address, phone, and fax number, here are just some of the items you might add to your e-mail signature:

- Brand logo
- Skype address
- Facebook fan page link
- Twitter link
- YouTube channel link
- Testimonials from a satisfied customer

- Link to a recent article or press release posted online
- Your photo (especially if you have customers in other cities)
- Information on latest product or service launch

What else could you include in your e-mail signature that would support your brand? Of course, you want to be careful not to make your e-mail signature too long, but don't hold back from including anything that differentiates you from your competition. And if your company has more than one person, be sure that everyone's e-mail signature looks the same. Remember: Consistency is key to building a strong brand!

Don't Let Your Brand Be a Weakling

What do you do if you discover that there's nothing all that "special" about your products or services?

Well, first of all, don't fret. As I said, there are plenty of ways to make a parity-performing product or service superior in the eyes of your customer — without being dishonest. For example, do you offer a money-back guarantee for your service or product? What kind of after-purchase services could you provide? How could your packaging and labeling be adjusted to come across more superior? How would you assess your staff or team performance? How flexible is your brand so that you can respond quickly to changing market needs? The answers to all of these questions can help you find meaningful points of difference vis-à-vis your customers.

Here's an exercise: Sit down and think about your brand's three biggest strengths and three biggest weaknesses. It's even more productive if you have a group of people helping you such as staff, loyal customers, friends, or family — people who know your brand well.

Get adhesive dots in two different colors, and gather everyone around. Brainstorm together until you have a list of your brand's potential strengths and weaknesses on a big piece of paper, and give every person three dots of each color. Choose one color to represent your brand's strengths and one color to represent its weaknesses. Then, ask everyone to place their dots next to what they consider to be the three strongest and weakest attributes of your brand. Finally, sit back as a group and see where there is consensus. This can be extremely eye-opening!

I've conducted this exercise in my workshops and spoken to dozens of business owners who have done the same exercise with their teams. The common strengths most brand leaders feel they offer are: (a) quality, (b) performance, and (c) value for money. If you feel the same about your brand, that's great! But I would also challenge you a bit and ask: How do you really know? If your customers praise you for these strengths regularly, then yes, you can be sure. Otherwise, how do you know—without a shadow of a doubt—that your quality and performance are truly strengths?

In Chapter 17, you will learn how important it is to assess your brand versus your competition. For now, if you haven't done this type of comparative analysis yet, you can't honestly be completely certain that your brand is as solid as you think.

For example, what about value for money? How do you know you're strong in that respect? Are you giving away products for free or simply offering your service at a very low price? Are you tracking your customers' perceptions of value over time? Remember: Value for money doesn't mean that your offerings have a low price; it means that even if your products or services are high priced, they're still worth the money. Mercedes Benz offers great value for the money for some. It's all about perception and the ongoing balance between price and performance.

Facing Your Weaknesses with Strength

In my workshops, the most common weakness—and greatest challenge—I hear about from SMEs and solo-preneurs is the lack of customer awareness. When I ask what that means, I get answers like: "We can't get buyers into the retail channels to look at our products seriously because there are just too many other alternatives," or "We have trouble getting people to know about the services we offer." If these issues are your biggest challenges, too, you've come to the right place! This book will continue to give you dozens more ideas about how to improve your customers' awareness of your brand without having to spend a lot of money.

The second biggest challenge business owners tell me they face is the ability to respond quickly to market needs. I often hear phrases like, "When you're busy trying to run a business, it's hard to look outside the box to see the next trend before it hits." What's the solution? Well, first, get out of the office (or warehouse or factory or wherever you normally work). Go where your customers are, network, join trade associations, read magazines and newspapers, surf the Internet for industry news, and buy trend reports. The more knowledgeable you are about what is going on in the market, the faster you will be able to pick up on new trends. And none of those ideas have to cost you a great deal of cash. You just need to invest some time.

The third biggest weakness I hear most often has to do with after-purchase services. I'm told: "We don't have the resources to build the right kind of system to handle after-purchase services," or "I don't even have a way to track who is buying my products, so how can I service them after they purchase?" or "I provide my service to my customer, they're happy with it, and that's the end of our interaction — why is there a need for follow-up?" When I hear this, my question in return is: How important are after-purchase services to ongoing customer satisfaction and the building of your brand? If these services are key, you need to make them a focus of your brand-building strategy.

Take a look at the strengths and weaknesses you believe are true of your brand, and ask yourself: "How do I *know* this is a weakness or a strength? What evidence do I have to support this belief?" If you don't have proof, you need to get it. Your brand is a combination of the perceptions, thoughts, and feelings that your customers have about it. So, what really matters is what *they* think, not what you think. Once again, remember: Marketing is all about the customer.

If you discover that your brand is strongest in an area that your customers don't care all that much about, those strengths are useless. Likewise, if your brand is weak in an area that your customers don't care much about, that weakness is insignificant and not worth addressing at all. So, as you assess your strengths and weaknesses, it's important to keep in mind what matters most to your Target Group.

Remember: Even if the products or services underlying your brand aren't the best in the market, what matters most is that your customers *believe* you're the best choice for them because you've created a meaningful point of difference.

16

WALKING, TALKING ADVERTISEMENTS

Brand-Building Asset #4 — Your Team

"Marketing is too important to be left to the marketing department."
— DAVID PACKARD, CO-FOUNDER OF HEWLETT-PACKARD

TIME AND AGAIN, I hear business owners say things like, "I only have a few team members on my staff — no one to focus solely on marketing," or "I'm a solo-preneur — just me, myself, and I — so I don't have any kind of marketing team to help me."

Branding Myth:
I don't have the staff I need to focus on marketing.

The truth is: Everybody's a marketer, and I'm here to tell you — and show you — that your marketing team is actually very large, even if you're a solo-preneur. So, there — another branding myth busted! Your marketing team actually includes *anybody who can spread the word about your brand.* Leveraged correctly and given the right tools, every single person you know (and every single person that *they* know) has the potential to become a cheerleader for your brand.

A phrase I coined some time ago is, "Every time you shake a hand, you market your brand." Think about it: The number of people you meet every day, every week, every month, and every year is sizeable. That's a lot of hand shaking and a lot of brand making. So, you don't have to have a marketing department or even a lot of employees to have a team of people who can effectively — and inexpensively — spread the word about your brand.

Growing Your Team

Still not convinced? I'm going to prove to you right now that your team is larger than you think. Sit down for a minute, grab a pen and paper, and brainstorm all of the "categories" of people you know. For example, a very small "section" of how I view my own marketing team list consists of:

- Current staff
- Vendors/suppliers
- Existing customers
- Coaching clients
- Association members
- Other entrepreneurs
- Booking agents in other countries
- Business school colleagues
- Subcontractors
- People who read my books (wink, wink)

Once you have that full list of categories, start to "fill in the blanks" by fleshing out the categories with specific individuals' names. When you're done with that, think of the various connections that those people have that can expand your marketing team even further. You will see your "marketing department" quickly increase from just a scattering of individuals to dozens, if not hundreds, of people.

Here are just a few more ideas of "categories" to consider:

- Immediate team members related to your business — everyone from ex-staff members to existing strategic partners to Twitter followers.
- Immediate team members from your personal life — think of friends and family members, as well as all of their connections.
- Outside team members who are related to your business — this might include consultants, advertisers, professional association members, reporters, bankers, landlords, and even your mail carriers.

- Outside team members from your personal life — this might include school alumni, community organizations you're involved in, doctors/dentists, and people involved in charities you support, just to name a few.

And the list goes on and on…

Hopefully, you can see how your "marketing team" really does consist of a large group of people, all willing and able to support your brand. What an asset!

Now, it's time to focus on how to leverage this incredible group of supporters.

You've Made Your List — What Now?

Once you have your full list written down, the #1 way to leverage this amazingly large marketing force is to make sure that the people on your team understand what your brand stands for. They need to be able to represent you well when they mention your brand to someone. Of course, this means that *you* need to be crystal clear first! But that shouldn't be a problem now that you have your Brand Positioning Statement in hand. If you need a refresher, refer back to your Statement or review page 97 of Chapter 12 to remind yourself how to summarize your positioning in a "nutshell."

Think about what your team members would say if someone stopped them on the street and asked them about your brand. Would they know how to talk about it in a way that truly reflects what you want your brand to stand for?

Don't Get "Stuck" on an Elevator!

You have no doubt heard of an "elevator speech." Well, I like to think of it as an "elevator brand introduction."

Imagine this: You enter an elevator on the 20th floor and push the ground floor button. As the elevator reaches the 19th floor, it stops, and a man gets on and says, "Hello." You think he could be an interesting business prospect. At best, you have about 20 seconds to speak and introduce your brand. What are you going to say?

I personally learned the hard way about not being prepared for this kind of situation. It was 2008, and I had just launched my first book.

In fact, the book had just been released two or three days before. I was at an author's convention and was carrying a copy of my book around with me. I got into an elevator, someone bumped into me, and the book fell out of my arms and onto the floor. A woman bent down, picked up the book, looked at the cover, and said, "Wow! Interesting title. Whose is this?" as she looked around the packed elevator. One glance at the woman, and I instantly realized who she was — the head of a major publishing company!

"It's mine," I replied.

Turning to look straight at me, she said, "Tell me more."

I was dumbstruck! I hadn't had time to think about my elevator brand introduction, and here I was facing this incredible opportunity! I remember fumbling through a general statement — I'm sure it wasn't particularly eloquent — and unfortunately, nothing ever came of it.

Tough lesson learned! You can bet I've never let that happen again. I sat down right away and perfected my elevator brand introduction for that particular book brand.

You never know what could come from an opportunity like this, so make sure you're prepared. Being ready with a concise and meaningful way to describe your brand is key.

Taking Your Brand Introduction on the Road

This type of brand introduction isn't only for elevators, of course. Think about the first question people usually ask when you meet them: "What do you do?" If you don't have a fast, engaging, crystal clear answer that communicates your brand, you've missed out on a potential chance to bring another marketing member onto your team.

Here are a few simple tips for creating a great elevator brand introduction:

1. Keep it short and concise — 20 seconds or less is best.

2. Don't just state your "job title"; describe what you do in a compelling way. "I'm an accountant" doesn't do much for your brand; in fact, it makes you sound just like everyone else — and that's no way to stand out in a crowd.

3. Describe who you do it for. Who are your customers/Target Group?

4. In your opening sentence (to grab the person's attention), describe the value, benefit, and quality that you bring to your customers in quantifiable terms — i.e., don't just say that you help your clients grow their businesses; say that you have helped X number of clients grow their businesses by XX% in a 12-month period. In other words, offer an example of what you have done for one or more customers.

5. Try to include information that will differentiate your brand from your competition. Using your Brand Positioning Statement, focus on the Benefits section. That's most likely what the potential customer will be interested in. Remember, they want to know what's in it for them!

Here are a few sample elevator brand introductions:

"I help families save money so that the kids can go to college and the parents can enjoy their retirement. I'm happy to say that, through my insurance and financial planning services, I've been able to save customers thousands of dollars every year. How about you — do you have children? … How many?" After receiving the answer: "How about we set up a time to talk about how I could help you pay for your children's education and still have money to retire?"

"I help women look and feel their best by not only providing them with great cosmetics but also by showing them how to apply the cosmetics beautifully. How about you? Which of your current cosmetics are you least satisfied with?" After receiving the answer: "I'd love to show you this great lipstick we have that lasts all day. When could we get together so that you could try it yourself?"

"I run my own human relations consulting business for small businesses. On average, I've been able to save my clients around $300 a year per employee while helping them keep their staff members for longer periods of time. What's your biggest issue with regard to employee hiring and retention?" After receiving the answer: "I've got some proven strategies for solving challenges like that. If you'd like, we could set up a time to talk about how I could help you adapt those strategies to your specific situation."

Once you have your elevator brand introduction written down and clearly stated, your team members need to become intimately aware of it — even memorize it — so that it flows easily from them, and they can represent your brand well. Why not make the learning process fun? For example, one SME client of mine made an entertaining afternoon out of this by taking his eight staff members up and down his office elevator, asking each individual to practice the company's elevator brand introduction. By the time they finished, every team member could introduce the brand easily in a way that was strategically consistent — and they had a lot of laughs in the process.

The #1 Under-Utilized Piece of "Branding Real Estate"

When you're introducing yourself on an elevator, it's not unusual to be asked for your business card. This little, seemingly innocuous piece of paper is one of the easiest, most effective — yet lowest cost — ways to build your brand. Unfortunately, far too many business owners overlook the significance of their cards and use them only to share the most basic of information. What a waste! That's why I call your business card the #1 under-utilized piece of "branding real estate" that exists.

Your business card should be working hard for you as a powerful brand-building tool. Grab one of your cards right now, and take a look at the front. You probably have the usual information there, but what do you include that powerfully reflects what your *brand* is all about? If you do have a lot of information there, is that information truly relevant? If you include a fax number, for example, how important is that to your business? Do your customers really use a fax anymore? Look objectively at the cover of your business card and assess its effectiveness.

Now (and here's the kicker), turn your business card over, and look at the back. If yours is like 80% of the business cards that have ever been handed to me, the back is *blank*! That's 50% of the available space on your card that's just sitting there waiting for you to use it to highlight your brand's point of differentiation. Don't let this branding faux pas happen to you.

"Back-Side Branding" . . . And I'm Not Talking Cattle

As I travel around the globe, I love to collect business cards that have broken the "mold" and effectively use the reverse side for brand-building purposes. Here are a few examples of what I call "back-side branding."

- Ogilvy Advertising Agency shows a map of the world, highlighting all of the cities where they have offices. It's a great way to support their global brand and to demonstrate that they can help companies with operations in numerous countries.

- One church in Southeast Asia helps new potential members find its locale easily by printing a mini map of the church's location on the back side of its card.

- A European wine distributor lists the various vineyards they represent.

- A flower shop in Singapore shares a full list of products and services it offers from customized arrangements for weddings, to plant care services, to gift baskets.

- A global company with a unique and distinctive trademark places that trademark on the back of their card and explains what it means as a way of solidifying their brand's Benefits.

- The back of a card from a real estate agent says, "The greatest compliment I can receive is a referral from my friends and clients." Considering what a powerful brand-booster a referral can be, this is a great way to subtly ask for one.

- A life coach includes a unique offer on the back of his business card. At the top, there's a line where he can write the name of the individual he has just met, and he signs it at the bottom. In the middle is a pre-printed offer for four free coaching sessions, effectively turning the back of his business card into a "trial coupon."

- One of my favorite examples is a card from a medium-sized business owner who runs a hospitality management company. Finding exceptional service providers is fundamental to the success of his brand, so he's always on the lookout for people who might fit that bill. If he's visiting a restaurant or a hotel, and a waiter or concierge offers him exceptional service, he hands them a card. On the front of the card are the words, "Thank you for your exceptional service." On the back, he lists all of the ways those service providers could contact him — if they happen to be in the market for a new job. It's a wonderfully "secretive" way of finding good service providers to work for him.

I've actually spent a lot of time thinking about my own business card and how it could best reflect my brand. In the end, I made my card four-sided. Since I have many clients around the world who never actually meet me in person, my business card is often their "first impression" of me when I mail them marketing materials. So, in addition to my logo, I put my photo on the front of the card, along with a simple statement about what Benefits my team and I offer. On the two inside flaps, I list the services my company provides and a brief bio of my background as a key credibility driver. Finally, on the back, I include standard contact information: official company name, address, phone numbers, e-mail, and website.

Of course, whatever you do, your business card — just like your storefront, your staff, and your Internet presence — must be consistent with your Brand Character! If you're a wild and creative graphic design artist, make sure that's reflected through the nature of your card. If your brand reflects a more serious professional services firm, make sure that comes through by the way your card "looks," as well. Remember: Brand consistency is important, and that applies even to brand-building tools as seemingly simple as your business card.

Another way to leverage your business card as a brand-builder is to hand out two or three business cards at a time. If you meet an interesting prospect, you can hand that person an extra card and say, "If you know of someone else who might also benefit from what I offer, I sure would appreciate you passing my card on to them."

Case in point: I own a Bose brand noise-reduction headset that I use when I fly. Inside the package that holds the headset, Bose has included five identical business cards that include information about the product and ways to contact Bose if someone is interested in buying a set. Think about it: If a fellow passenger on a plane asks me about the headset, all I have to do is hand them one of those cards. Smart!

One word of caution with regard to business cards, however: Be careful that you don't list too many "specializations." The back of one card I collected lists 32 different types of services that this one firm provides. Everything from education planning to insurance claims to secretarial services! That kind of "throw the net wide" approach doesn't create a brand — it defeats it.

I'm reminded of an old cartoon that shows a man at a stand with a sign that reads, "Joe's Landfill and Croissants." If what you do is too diverse or too much for your customers to keep straight, you will confuse them rather than further your brand. So, as I've mentioned before, you need to make some tough choices. That's part and parcel of the proper care and feeding of a brand.

Last but not least, make sure that everyone on your team has a business card — and I mean everyone! If you own a small hotel, everyone from the manager to the concierge to the housekeeping staff to the busboy should have a card with your brand's Benefits clearly stated. After all, as I've said, they are indeed walking, talking advertisements for your brand, day in and day out.

Your Team's Marketing Mindset

Horst Schulze, the former COO and President of the Ritz-Carlton chain of hotels, knew that his guests were demanding, high-income clients, so he made sure that his entire staff had a specific marketing mindset. He empowered everyone from managers to busboys to house-keepers to provide exceptional service by letting them know they had the authorization to spend up to $2,000 per customer to keep that individual happy or to solve any problem a hotel guest might have.

How well did this work? Here's a true story to illustrate.

A businessman staying at the Ritz-Carlton hotel in Atlanta, Georgia, packed his bag, checked out, and took a taxi to the Atlanta airport to fly to Honolulu, where he was to give a presentation at a conference. When he reached into his bag at the airport's security checkpoint, he suddenly realized he had left his laptop at the hotel. Panicked, he picked up his cell phone, called the Ritz-Carlton, and asked to be put through to housekeeping. "I think I left my laptop in my room," he said. "Can you please check?" he asked. A few anxious moments later, the housekeeper returned to the phone and confirmed, "Yes, sir, I do have your laptop."

He quickly responded, "Okay, here's what I need you to do. Please FedEx the computer to me overnight. I'm speaking at a conference, so it's critical that you get it to me in Honolulu by tomorrow." He gave her the address where he would be staying and hung up.

As you can imagine, during the long flight to Honolulu, the businessman's nerves were on edge, wondering what would happen if his laptop didn't arrive in time for his presentation at 2:00 p.m. the next day.

Fast forward to 10:00 a.m. the next morning in Honolulu. Pacing the floor in his hotel room, the businessman finally heard a knock. He held his breath, hoping it was the FedEx delivery person. Instead, when he opened the door, there stood ... the housekeeper from the Ritz-Carlton in Atlanta! She handed him the laptop and said, "It was just too important. I couldn't take a chance it wouldn't get to you on time."

Now, I ask you: Do you think this man will ever stay at any other hotel than a Ritz-Carlton?

(Of course, that housekeeper was no fool — she *did* get a free trip to Honolulu...)

The Corporate Brand/Personal Brand Connection

What I love about that story is that Horst Schulze put in place a system that allowed the members of his team to communicate Ritz-Carlton's corporate brand and also express their individual *personal* brands in a way that was consistent with the values of the hotel chain. It allowed for a perfect "fit," creating what I call a powerful "Corporate Brand/ Personal Brand Connection.™" Imagine how satisfied the employees of Ritz-Carlton must be as a result of experiencing this connection and having this level of empowerment. And imagine how much this practice has increased the hotel's employee retention over the years, too.

In fact, each person working at the Ritz is expected to carry a business card in their pocket, which includes the hotel's credo on the back: "We are Ladies and Gentlemen Serving Ladies and Gentlemen." If you ask any employee at Ritz-Carlton for their card, they'll pull it out of their pocket and show it to you.

This doesn't just represent a marketing mindset; it's an entire operating system that empowers the staff to reflect what the Ritz-Carlton brand stands for through their individual actions. How could you apply this concept to *your* brand?

What Are Your Existing Customers Worth?

As I mentioned before, studies show that it costs anywhere from six to nine times more to attract a new customer than to keep an existing customer happy. How much are your clients/customers worth to you? How much would you spend to keep them happy? Let's bring this to life with some numbers.

Invest some time to calculate the lifetime value of your average customer:

1. Take your average sales transaction value.
2. Multiply that by the number of times an average customer buys your brand during any given year.
3. Multiply the outcome by the typical number of years a satisfied customer could stick with your brand.

The result represents the estimated lifetime value of an average client.

Let's use a graphic designer as an example. Assume the average customer spends $750 on a design project and carries out three projects a year. That means the yearly value of one customer is $750 x 3, or $2,250. Now, multiply that by, say, 15 years, and you see the lifetime value of that one client is actually $34,000!

How would the graphic designer's team members act differently if they knew that every customer who placed an order was potentially worth $34,000? Since that number most likely represents a sizable chunk of an employee's salary, I suspect it would make a big difference in how team members view — and treat — customers. So, take out that calculator, crunch the numbers, and get clear on how much your customers are worth to the growth of your brand. Then, make sure everyone on your team understands this value and reflects it appropriately in their interactions with clients.

Get Your Team Fired Up!

Involving your team — large or small — in marketing and branding activities will not only net you some potentially great ideas, but will give everyone a vested interest in how well your brand performs in the marketplace. And it's a lot of fun, too! Here are some ways you can engage everyone you know in brand building:

- **Brainstorm Marketing and Branding Ideas as a Group**. Assemble a team, buy them pizza, and just go for it. You might even have a contest for the best idea that is most consistent with what you want your brand to stand for. The prize could be something as simple as going home an hour early on Friday, a free product or service, or a gift like a bottle of wine.

- **Create a Marketing Suggestion Box.** Big companies do this with tremendous success. Since everyone is a marketer, your marketing ideas can come from anyone, and your team will appreciate that you're giving them a chance to contribute.

- **Offer Incentives to Bring in New Business.** For team members who work for you, you could offer a percentage of profits or some other kind of bonus. It doesn't have to cost much, but what you offer will be worth it when you consider what you'll earn from a new customer. Thinking beyond employees and staff, you can offer a finder's fee of some kind or develop a reciprocal referral relationship with colleagues and others who don't work directly with you.

- **Create a Library Filled with Great Marketing and Branding Books.** Encourage your team to learn more about the topic. If you'd like some suggestions, some recommended books are listed at the back of the book to get you and your team started.

Your Brand's First Touch Point

The old saying, "You never get a second chance to make a first impression" holds particularly true when it comes to building a strong brand. If a potential customer's very first touch point doesn't represent your brand the way you want, you may never get another opportunity.

What is your brand's first "touch point" with a potential brand loyalist? Just who — or what — makes up your "frontline"? Is it the receptionist who greets customers as they come through the door? Is it the operator who answers the phone? Is it your Facebook page, your tweets on Twitter, or your storefront? Or is your website a new customer's first line of contact for which you and the IT team are responsible?

Sometimes, the answer to "who makes your brand's first impression" may surprise you. For example, in the hotel industry, it's rare that you will run into the general manager. In reality, the folks you run into most often are the bellmen, the cleaning team, and the front desk staff, right?

So, you need to be clear about who (or what) makes your brand's first impression, and make sure those "walking, talking advertisements" know how to represent your brand in the best possible way.

Consider this even if you are a solo-preneur, and you use a virtual office as your "receptionist/secretary." When we started our first Asian office, we used a virtual office to answer and forward phone calls. A few weeks into it, a major multinational client complained about the person who answered the phone because he couldn't understand her. I called to check on it and discovered that the virtual office's staff didn't always speak English very well! So, from that moment on, we insisted that only fluent English speakers answer our overseas phones.

After that, we carefully checked out any outside resources we used to represent our brand, and we didn't become complacent about it. We regularly called our virtual office just to "test" how the calls were being answered. I have always been grateful to the client who was willing to speak up and tell me about the problem. If he hadn't done so, I might never have known, and it could have seriously damaged our brand.

The moral of the story? First, know exactly who or what constitutes your customers' first touch points with your brand, and second, make sure the people, website, or materials that represent your brand are doing so exactly as you want. Otherwise, you are not only missing a great brand-building opportunity, but you may be accidentally damaging your brand and losing valuable customers without realizing it.

17

KEEP YOUR CUSTOMERS CLOSE AND YOUR COMPETITION CLOSER

Brand-Building Asset #5 — Your Competitors

"Your most dangerous competitors are those that are most like you."
— BRUCE HENDERSON, FOUNDER OF THE
BOSTON CONSULTING GROUP

BUSINESS OWNERS OFTEN SAY TO ME, "Brenda, there's no way our competitors are brand-building assets. They're more like liabilities!" Well, I'm here to tell you that nothing could be further from the truth.

That's yet another branding myth busted! The truth is that your competition can help you build your brand more than you ever imagined. You can — in fact, you must — leverage your competition if you want to create and grow a strong brand presence. That may seem counter-intuitive but, in this chapter, I'm going to show you why and how.

Here's the deal: You need to know your competitors as well as you know your own business. Think about it... what do professional athletes do before a big game or match? They watch previously recorded games of their opponents. Why? Sports teams know that analyzing their opponents' moves, approaches, and tactics in different plays will help them carve out the best strategies for winning.

As a business owner, you need to take similar action to analyze and understand your own competition. In fact, by using information about your competition the same way professional athletes do, your competition can become one of your most powerful brand-building assets.

You Can't Win Unless You Know Who Could Beat You

Now, you may be thinking, "But, Brenda, I already know a lot about my competition." Fair point, and indeed, you might. But my challenge to you is: Do you really? Consider your top two or three fiercest competitors. On a scale of 1 to 10 — "10" means you know these competitors like the back of your hand, and "1" means you don't know them at all — what score would you give yourself?

Don't feel bad if your self-assessment is low on the scale. If you're like a lot of SME owners and solo-preneurs I know, there's a tendency to focus primarily on building your own brand. After all, that's enough to fill your plate, right? Many smaller business owners have said to me, "Brenda, get real! I don't have the time or money to get to know my competition better." But you don't have to create a 30-page analysis on each of your competitors like multinational brands do. Just by spending a few hours a month, you can become keenly aware of what your competitors are doing, and it doesn't have to cost much.

Become a Modern-Day Sherlock Holmes

Here are some low-cost and no-cost ways to build your brand by getting to know your competition better:

Clippings. To stay up to date on what is going on with their competitors, big businesses often hire a "clipping service." They pay people to read carefully through newspapers and magazines and clip any articles they find about their competition. But who wants to spend a lot of money to do that? Instead, why not designate one person on your team to look through the newspaper and local magazines for information about your competing companies?

If you're a solo-preneur without a staff or your Target Group extends beyond your local market, set up a Google Alert for your competition. All you have to do is go to www.Google.com/alert, put in the name of your competitor, and Google does the rest by sending you a link to any information that's posted about that particular competitor once a day, once a week — as often as you'd like. (And, by the way, you should also set up an alert for your own brand so you can stay on top of what others are posting about you!)

Subscribe. Sign up to receive your competitors' mailings. This includes any online newsletters, RSS feeds, YouTube channels, and blogs.

Follow. Look for your competitors' accounts on Facebook and Twitter. Follow them or "like" their Facebook pages, and read their tweets and updates periodically. If you feel more comfortable using your personal e-mail address than your professional address for this type of thing, that's up to you to decide. The key is to stay on top of what's happening with your competition.

Reward Your Team for Information. Establish a system for rewarding team members who bring you helpful information about your competitors. No, I'm not talking about rewarding someone for becoming a spy or infiltrating a competitor's organization! Simply ask your staff and your extended marketing team (that you discovered in Chapter 16) to keep their eyes and ears open for information that's readily available and to share it regularly with you.

Here's a personal example: Years ago, when I worked at Procter & Gamble in Poland managing the company's hair care brands, 26 new shampoo brands were launched in a single year! It was part of our team's job to keep tabs on all of them, but there was so much going on that we decided to set up a reward system for the sales team to bring in any information they could find about these new brands. After all, the salespeople were in the market day in and day out, so they were most likely to be aware of what these competitive brands were doing. The incentive was company-wide recognition, so our salespeople really got into it. It culminated in year-end awards when we honored one particular salesperson with the "best competitive information" award. It was a coveted honor among the sales team, and we got the exact type of competitive information we needed.

Take Seminars. If a competitor is giving a teleseminar or webinar, sign up. This is becoming an increasingly popular way for small service businesses to market themselves, and it gives you an opportunity to understand these competing brands' offerings better.

Use Competing Products and Services. Yes, that's right. Nothing will tell you more about the quality of your competitors' brands than using their products and services yourself.

A few years back, I was training some Marketing team members at a company that manufactured and sold yoghurt. I asked them how their competitive brands compared with their own product, only to discover that it was against that company's policy to eat a competitor's yogurt! How can you set a strategy to win if you don't know how well you compare to the other brands your Target Group could choose?

I nipped that limiting rule in the bud, right then and there. We got out of our chairs, marched to the nearest convenience store, bought some competitive yogurt brands, came back to the training room, and ate them. As a result of that experience, the team realized that their product was actually of higher quality than their competition, but their packaging was inferior. This began a whole packaging change project, which helped them build a better brand experience for their customers. But they would never have known it was necessary if they hadn't tried other yogurts.

I once stayed at a Sheraton hotel where I had the opportunity to talk with the manager about how they stay up to date on what their competition is doing. He told me that all of their senior leaders are required to stay at competing hotels one night each year, keeping track of everything from the experience of making a reservation, to checking in, to ordering room service, to using the pool and health club. They are expected to book a tour through the concierge, write down the contents of the mini-bar, bring back all of the complimentary toiletries — everything. The next day, all of the leaders get together in a big conference room and discuss what they learned. Obviously, this practice costs them some money, but it provides a wealth of information. What similar, yet less costly, ways could you employ to find out about your competitors?

Follow My "Brand-Builder's Golden Rule"

As you gather your information, take heed of my brand-builder's "golden rule":

Find out what your competition is doing *right*, then do it better.

Don't jump too quickly to denigrate your competition. It's too easy to say, "My competitors are no good." If you actively search for what they're doing right, you'll unearth much more valuable information. Remember: Even though you may not think your competitors are any good, their customers obviously see it differently. Think like a loyal user of that particular brand. What does that person see in your competitor's brand that you don't?

Some people say to me, "Gosh, Brenda, I don't know… isn't this spying?" Absolutely not — that's yet another branding myth busted! This isn't about infiltrating your competitor's organization looking for secrets. Nothing I've recommended is illegal. You're simply researching information about key brands from sources that are readily available.

Let's be clear: I'm definitely not encouraging any kind of illegal or unethical behavior. In fact, I have a painful personal story about this kind of inappropriate behavior that relates to my own business. A colleague and I were hired by the marketing director of a large company to conduct marketing training for them. The marketing director seemed to be in a big hurry to get the training done quickly, and I didn't understand why until I found out four days after we had conducted the course that this same director left that company to start her own marketing training company! Unfortunately, I also discovered that she was using our training materials. This is not the kind of thing I'm advocating. Don't steal your competitors' ideas. Instead, use the information you find to make your brand better.

By the way, don't kid yourself — your competitors are probably investigating your brand in the exact same way. This is simply a natural approach to understanding more about the brands you're up against. You owe it to yourself, your team, your company, and your brand to do the same.

The Six Elements of Your Competitors' Positioning

Key to the success of your own brand is having a clear understanding of your competitors' brand positioning, too — that particular piece of real estate in the customer's mind that your competitor is trying to own. But how do you get that? Picking up the phone, calling your competition, and saying, "Could I see your Brand Positioning Statement?" probably isn't going to work. But what you *can* do is infer their Brand Positioning Statements by analyzing their brands in the same way you analyzed your own.

Stop for a moment, and think about one of your favorite brands. I'll bet if you sat down and focused on it, you could infer a Positioning Statement for that brand based on what you already know, couldn't you? You can do the same with your competitors' brands.

All sorts of information is available to fully understand your competitors, so go ahead and give it a try. Choose a key competitor, and gather as much information as you can. Look at that competitor's website, check out any advertising they might have (handout flyers, magazine ads, radio, even television). Review their price list, brochures, newsletters, press releases, and articles. If the brand is sold in retail outlets, look at examples of their in-store merchandising. Check out their Facebook page, their blog, their listing with the Better Business Bureau, any YouTube videos they have posted, and what you can find out about them through the various search engines. Once you've gathered all of this information, use it to work through the six elements of their Brand Positioning Statement:

1. **Target Market**—Who is this competitor's targeted customer in terms of demographics and psychographics? How does that customer feel about the particular product or service category? How does that customer feel about that specific competitor?

2. **Needs**—What are their customers' Needs, and how does that competitive brand fill those Needs—both functional and emotional?

3. **Competitive Framework**—Who does this competitor see as *their* competitors, and how do they differentiate their own brand from those competitors?

4. **Benefits**—What key functional and emotional Benefits does their brand promise to customers? How do they use their Benefits to distinguish their brand from others?

5. **Reasons Why**—What Reasons Why does this competitor give their customers to believe that their brand can deliver those Benefits?

6. **Brand Character**—What is the personality or "attitude" of the competitor's brand? If this brand were a person, how would you describe that person?

Once you've done this analysis, create an "Inferred Positioning Statement" for your competitor's brand, writing down each of the six positioning elements for that competitor based on what you see and understand. Then, once you have your Inferred Positioning Statement for the key competitor, place it side by side with your own Positioning Statement. You'll be surprised how much you can learn by doing this type of comparison.

As you review both your statement and your competitor's, here are some questions to consider:

- Do you and your competitor have similar or different Target Groups?

- How different are your functional and emotional Needs? Does your brand fill a customer Need that your competitor doesn't, or does your competitor's brand fill a Need that yours doesn't?

- Is *your* brand on this competitor's radar screen? If not, why not?

- What Benefits does your competitor's brand offer that are similar or different from yours? What Benefits can your brand own that this competitor can't? Do you promote that Benefit enough in your own marketing communications?

- What Reasons Why does your competitor use in their marketing efforts that are stronger or weaker than yours? Put yourself in the shoes of your Target Group, and judge for yourself: Which brand would you buy based on each specific brand's Reasons Why?

- How does your competitor's Brand Character speak to your Target Group, and how does it compare to yours?

This is an incredibly eye-opening exercise that can give you a much better idea of where your brand stands in comparison to the other options your customers have. Use this opportunity to go back and visit your own Brand Positioning Statement. Ask yourself: Which of the six elements could you strengthen in your own positioning in order to become the preferred brand of choice for your customers?

Just How Powerful Is This Exercise?

One company I know did this analysis, comparing their brand with their top competitor. After they had gathered all of the information and created an Inferred Brand Positioning Statement for the competition, it became clear that their own brand's Benefits and Reasons Why were almost an exact replica of that competitor. Ouch! It was a painful lesson, but it helped them understand better why they were constantly competing neck-and-neck with this competitor's brand, never becoming the preferred brand for the majority of their Target Group.

So, what did they do? They didn't think they could change their core Benefits, but they decided to develop new, distinctive, and more compelling Reasons Why that would give them an edge over this key competitor. They found a well-known and strategically meaningful industry association to endorse their brand in all of their marketing activities. It didn't take long for this new brand strategy to have an impact, and their sales soon began to show it.

Moral of the story? Know your competitors' positionings as well as you know your own, and you can set a true course to win in the marketplace.

18

Smarter Branding You Can Bank On

A Few Final Words

"Great brands don't become great by accident."
— Brenda Bence, International Branding
Expert and Coach

You did it! You have covered all five of the inexpensive but effective assets you already have to build your brand. I hope you can see now how you can leverage each one of these to improve and strengthen your own unique position in the marketplace. And you can do it immediately, no matter the state of the economy, no matter how big or small your budget, and regardless of how much time, people, or ideas you have. You now have a veritable treasure chest of proven low-cost or no-cost resources that you can use for smarter branding... starting now.

Holding On to Your Mindset

Of course, it's critical to stay in your marketing mindset, but I know it's difficult. The demands of running your own show and meeting the Needs of existing customers can often mean that marketing and branding are relegated to the back burner. So, how do you keep brand-building top of mind?

- One of my clients has carved out time on her calendar every day from 10:00 a.m. to 11:00 a.m. to focus solely on branding and marketing activities.

- Another of my clients keeps a crystal paperweight made up of his brand's logo in the middle of his desk, and every time he looks at it, he's reminded to ask himself what he's done to market his brand that day.

What would it take for you to do something similar? If you don't have the time to do some marketing and branding activities every day, what could you achieve if you devoted half an hour every *other* day? And how about your extended marketing team? How often could you set up a marketing lunch to discuss and brainstorm new marketing ideas? Once a month? Once a quarter? Set some goals and then, to keep yourself on track, consider enlisting an "accountability buddy" — someone who will make sure you follow through on your marketing and branding action plans.

Focus On Your Assets

To help you maintain that important marketing mindset, regularly review the five core assets that you already have to build your brand:

Asset #1: *Positioning* — Refer to your completed Brand Positioning Statement every day, and make sure that each action you take is 100% aligned with the positioning you want to own in the market.

Asset #2: *Your Customers* — Use the dozens of ideas you have now uncovered to build your brand bigger and better through leveraging your existing customers.

Asset #3: *Your Products and Services* — Create a truly meaningful point of difference for your products and services that you can use daily to help set your brand apart.

Asset #4: *Your Team* — Leverage your newly-expanded "marketing department" so that they become walking, talking advertisements for your brand.

Asset #5: *Your Competition* — Know your competition well enough to confirm you have a differentiated place in the market.

The Bottom Line

As I've said before, there are really two fundamental steps to building a powerhouse brand:

1. Be crystal clear about what you want your brand to stand for.

2. Communicate that desired brand consistently, consistently, consistently every single day in everything you do.

Great brands don't become great brands by accident! So, don't just sit there. Create an action plan, and enlist members of your staff/extended marketing team to help you execute the plan. Write down each important task, and track how your plan is progressing by capturing:

- The specific activity to do
- Who is responsible for that activity
- Date by which that activity will be completed
- What success for that activity will look like

Then, assign an accountability buddy who is responsible for helping ensure the activity is completed on time.

A strong brand for you *is* in reach, so no more excuses! You know what it takes, and you have the resources. If you find yourself falling into that "I can't do it" mode again, be sure to keep a paperclip around to remind you of what is possible.

• • • •

I hope this book has been helpful for you and that you're excited about the possibilities for building your brand. If you want to stay in touch and get regular updates on how to build a stronger brand for yourself, your products and services, and your company, visit www.brendabence.com/enewsletter and sign up for my *Successful Branding* e-newsletter.

If you want to build a powerhouse brand faster and earn even greater profits for less money, check out our accelerated program, *Fast Track to Smarter Branding™ — The Ultimate Package.* This one-of-a-kind course is filled with advanced tools and tips to help you quickly gain additional marketing skills, build a more resilient and sustainable brand, and boost your bottom line. It contains:

- *Smarter Branding Without Breaking the Bank* in three handy versions: e-book for digital viewing on any type of screen; audio book for your MP3 player; and paperback

- Accompanying workbook with customizable brand-building worksheets in both hard copy and fill-in-the-blank PDF format

- 20 Video Learning Sessions (5 hours in total) in which I share expert instruction, insider secrets, success stories, and dozens more smarter branding examples

- 52 new, unique, and actionable *Smarter Branding* tips sent directly to your e-mail inbox every week for a year

- A no-questions-asked, money-back satisfaction guarantee. There's nothing to lose!

Visit www.Smarter-Branding.com to find out more.

I'd also love to receive your feedback. What parts of *Smarter Branding Without Breaking the Bank* have helped you most? What questions do you still have? This kind of input helps us improve our brand as well, so we really appreciate it.

Here are a couple of different ways you can share your feedback with us:

- Send an e-mail to: Feedback@Smarter-Branding.com

- Submit your feedback online at: www.Smarter-Branding.com/feedback

Lastly, of course, if you have enjoyed this book, I would certainly appreciate you recommending it to others. We've talked about the value of referrals, so thank you in advance for yours.

Here's to smarter branding without breaking the bank!

ABOUT THE AUTHOR

Brenda S. Bence is Founder and President of BDA (Brand Development Associates) International Ltd., a firm that specializes in helping companies and individual clients around the world build successful, growth-oriented corporate and personal brands. As a Certified Speaking Professional, Certified Executive Coach, and dynamic trainer and consultant, Brenda has worked with hundreds of executives, managers, and entrepreneurs around the world to help them define and communicate their  corporate and personal brands. Brenda spends the majority of the year traveling to present her unique approach to branding at conferences, conventions, and corporations all across the globe.

Having earned her MBA from Harvard Business School, Brenda began her career as a marketer at Procter & Gamble, first at P&G's world headquarters in the U.S., then with P&G in Europe and in Asia. She subsequently held the position of Vice President International Marketing for Bristol-Myers Squibb's consumer division, Mead Johnson, where Brenda was responsible for multiple brands across almost 50 countries.

During her 25-year career, Brenda has helped manage dozens of well-known brands, including Pantene, Vidal Sassoon Shampoo & Styling products, Head & Shoulders, Enfamil, Choc-o-Milk, and Ariel and Cheer Laundry Detergents, just to name a few.

Happily married to her husband, Daniel, for the past 13 years, Brenda splits her time between homes in Singapore and the U.S. She also sits on a number of boards of public and private companies and not-for-profit organizations. See www.BrendaBence.com.

FAST TRACK TO SMARTER BRANDING™ — THE ULTIMATE PACKAGE

Now that you've read *Smarter Branding Without Breaking the Bank,* you've learned how to build a strong brand using the resources you already have. Would you now like to earn even bigger profits for less money — in less time?

Fast Track to Smarter Branding™ — The Ultimate Package is an accelerated learning program that will bring you the advanced tools and tips you need to build a powerhouse brand even faster. Here's what you get:

- *Smarter Branding Workbook,* in both hard copy and fill-in-the-blank PDF format, with dozens of worksheets and exercises that you can customize to your own brand and business.

- *20 Video Learning Sessions (5 hours in total).* It's like having Brenda as your personal branding and marketing tutor in the comfort of your home or office. Includes expert instruction, insider secrets, mega-brand strategies at work in smaller businesses — and much more.

- *52 New, Unique, and Actionable Smarter Branding Tips* sent directly to your e-mail inbox — one every week for a year. Stay informed, inspired, and in control with fresh, low-cost branding ideas you can use immediately.

- *Smarter Branding Without Breaking the Bank* in e-book format to download and use on any screen, audiobook format read by Brenda and downloadable to your MP3 player, and in paperback.

- *Our No-Questions-Asked, Money-Back Satisfaction Guarantee.* You have nothing to lose!

Shift your brand-building into overdrive.
Order at www.Smarter-Branding.com.

Smarter Branding Without Breaking the Bank in paperback, e-book and audiobook formats

20 Video Learning Sessions taught by Brenda Bence

52 Smarter Branding Tips sent to your inbox, a new tip every week for a year

Easy-to-use workbook both in hard copy and fill-in-the-blank digital format

Acknowledgments

When something can be read without effort, great effort has gone into its writing.

— Enrique Jardiel Poncela

Based on that quote — and on the "great effort" that has gone into *Smarter Branding Without Breaking the Bank* — this book should be a very easy read! All kidding aside, I certainly hope you have found it a breeze to understand and digest.

The truth is that years and years of work have gone into writing *Smarter Branding*, and as with any book, it is never just one person who makes it happen. Many thanks to the following individuals who have lent their considerable talents to help this book come to fruition:

- Melanie Votaw who has had the patience and persistence to edit all of my books over the years
- George Foster for terrific cover design and consistent willingness to keep working at it until it's right
- Eric Myhr for his fantastic sense of humor and outstanding typesetting services
- Graham Dixhorn for his expert cover-writing skills
- Swas Siripong "Kwan" for quick and excellent graphic design development
- Emily Ross for her sharp mind, excellent research support, and some good laughs along the way
- Richard Czerniawski and Michael Maloney from Brand Development Network International (BDNI) for their excellent branding collaboration over the years

I am also very grateful to all *Smarter Branding Without Breaking the Bank* participants who have attended my workshops over the years and shared their brand-building stories. Without them, this book would definitely not be as rich.

Besides those who actually worked "on" the book, there were many key people who cheered me on throughout the process of book development. My sincere gratitude goes to:

Daniel, my partner in life and in business. I wouldn't want to go through this journey with anyone else!

The entire staff at Brand Development Associates International for their support and patience during the writing and development of *Smarter Branding*.

My Team, thank you for your unwavering support.

SUGGESTED BOOKS

Competitive Positioning: Best Practices for Creating Brand Loyalty, Richard D. Czerniawski & Michael W. Maloney, 2011

The 22 Immutable Laws of Branding, Al Ries and Laura Ries, 2002

Brand Warfare, David D'Alessandro, 2001

How YOU™ are like Shampoo, Brenda Bence, 2008

Rising Tide: Lessons from 165 Years of Brand Building at Procter & Gamble, Davis Dyer, Frederick Dalzell, and Rowena Olegario, 2004

Emotional Branding : How Successful Brands Gain the Irrational Edge, Daryl Travis, 2000

B2B Brand Management, Philip Kotler and Waldemar Pfoertsch, 2006